The Julian Way

MISSIONAL WISDOM LIBRARY
RESOURCES FOR CHRISTIAN COMMUNITY

The Missional Wisdom Foundation experiments with and teaches about alternative forms of Christian community. The definition of what constitutes a Christian community is shifting as many seek spiritual growth outside of the traditional confines of church. Christians are experimenting with forming communities around gardens, recreational activities, coworking spaces, and hundreds of other focal points, connecting with their neighbors while being aware of the presence of God in their midst. The Missional Wisdom Library series includes resources that address these kinds of communities and their cultural, theological, and organizational implications.

Series Editor: Larry Duggins

Forthcoming titles

The Julian Way

A Theology of Fullness
for All of God's People

Justin Hancock

Foreword by Jeremy Schipper

CASCADE *Books* • Eugene, Oregon

THE JULIAN WAY
A Theology of Fullness for All of God's People

Missional Wisdom Library: Resources for Christian Community 6

Cascade Books
An Imprint of Wipf and Stock Publishers
199 W. 8th Ave., Suite 3
Eugene, OR 97401

www.wipfandstock.com

PAPERBACK ISBN: 978-1-5326-1159-9
HARDCOVER ISBN: 978-1-5326-1161-2
EBOOK ISBN: 978-1-5326-1160-5

Cataloguing-in-Publication data:

Names: Hancock, Justin, author. | Schipper, Jeremy, foreword.

Title: The julian way : a theology of fullness for all of God's people / Justin Hancock ; foreword by Jeremy Schipper.

Description: Eugene, OR : Cascade Books, 2018 | Missional Wisdom Library: Resources for Christian Community 6 | Includes bibliographical references.

Identifiers: ISBN 978-1-5326-1159-9 (paperback) | ISBN 978-1-5326-1161-2 (hardcover) | ISBN 978-1-5326-1160-5 (ebook)

Subjects: LCSH: Theological anthropology—Christianity. | People with disabilities—Religious aspects—Christianity. | Church work with people with disabilities.

Classification: BV4460 .H36 2018 (print) | BV4460 .H36 (ebook)

Manufactured in the U.S.A.   JUNE 7, 2018

To my wife, for being my best friend, my biggest supporter, and my greatest source of strength. I love you always.

Table of Contents

TABLE OF CONTENTS

Foreword

I WOULD LIKE TO thank Justin for inviting me to write a foreword
to his project. I do not self-identify as a theologian or a church
historian, so I will leave it to others to assess the theological spe-
cifics of this project. Nevertheless, I want to be very clear about
this project's starting point because it reflects a simple fact that
most of the theological treatments of disability that I have come
across, including those of the theologians that Justin engages in
the following pages, cannot seem to account for: Justin Hancock
is proud of his Cerebral Palsy. Early on in this work, he writes,
"My Cerebral Palsy is a struggle. It's also something I am very, very
proud of. I invite the church to live with us and know us as people."
This invitation to the church represents one of the primary goals
of Justin's project. Yet, no one can "live with and know" Justin if
they are unaware of his CP pride. Justin does not say that he is
proud of the ways that he has struggled with, managed, or overcome his Cerebral Palsy. He does not say that he is proud of his
many accomplishments or the ways that he has thrived while living with Cerebral Palsy. Instead, he simply claims to be proud of
his Cerebral Palsy.

Justin claims this CP pride without qualification or apology.
He does not argue that the fact that one has Cerebral Palsy means
that one has a unique contribution to offer the church as a member, as a leader, as a sermon illustration, or even as a theological
metaphor for the church, the latter of which unfortunately serves
as a foundational aspect of some of the theological projects he

engages. (Such metaphors only work if, as with the medical model, one isolates disability from the social or cultural contexts emphasized in disability rights and liberation movements and in disability studies.) Justin never justifies, explains, or defends his CP pride. It is simply assumed. For example, when discussing how Dietrich Bonhoeffer's work can contribute to a conversation that Justin feels is necessary within disabled communities, he writes, "In order for those in the disabled community to claim their rightful place in community with one another and in the larger theological and cultural conversation, it is not necessary that we abandon our pride in our unique disabled situations, but disability can no longer be the starting point and the center piece of our reality." Here, Justin is addressing an in-group conversation among folks with disabilities rather than members of the dominant culture within the larger Church. Notice the way he characterizes the attitudes of folks of disabilities toward our "unique disabled situations." It is not characterized as shameful and bitter or romanticized as courageous and inspirational or by any of the other common stereotypes frequently mapped onto our situations. Instead, Justin assumes that it is a source of pride that should not be abandoned. For Justin, it is simply a given that one can be, and is, proud of one's Cerebral Palsy.

He again references his CP pride when he discusses rivalries and hierarchies of disability within disabled communities. These occur between physical vs. cognitive disabilities, visible vs. invisible disabilities, acquired vs. congenital disabilities, and so on. While addressing these concerns, he writes, "I will be the first to admit that when I have the opportunity to get together with a number of people with Cerebral Palsy within a larger disabled group, I tend to gravitate towards those with CP because of our common experience and pride in our situation." Once again, Justin makes a passing reference to being proud of Cerebral Palsy. I imagine that he does not elaborate on this passing reference because it is simply a given. For those who share this pride in their Cerebral Palsy, it does not need to be explained or defended.

CP Pride is beyond doubt for Justin. In fact, he makes this perfectly clear when he writes that it is "beyond doubt (at least to me) that my Cerebral Palsy has done much to inform my character as an individual and has become a proud part of who I continue to grow to be, both as a man and in the context of my relationship with Jesus Christ." Cerebral Palsy is rarely associated with notions of masculinity, in part because of a tendency to infantilize and desexualize males with Cerebral Palsy or distance us from common stereotypes of masculine behavior within the dominant culture, including, but not limited to, self-control or autonomy. By contrast, Justin's Cerebral Palsy shapes not only his religious commitments but his masculinity. It is a proud part of what makes him a man. Early on in this work, he describes me as not only an employed biblical scholar but as "a man living with the daily reality of Cerebral Palsy." I was struck by this description because, while I have frequently been described in print with career-first language ("a scholar with Cerebral Palsy") or person-first language ("a person with Cerebral Palsy"), this is the first time that I can remember that someone described me as a man with Cerebral Palsy.

Although Justin and I became friends as grown men, I imagine that Justin's self-described relationship with Jesus Christ developed in the Christian home in which he was raised. Although this is not always the case, one very often learns in the home how to negotiate one's religious identity within the dominant culture—whether or not that aspect of one's identity is privileged by the dominant culture. Yet, if they are raised in the home, the vast majority of folks with Cerebral Palsy are brought up by non-disabled parents or family members. For example, I never knew any adults with Cerebral Palsy until after I left for college. For males with Cerebral Palsy, this means that we often have to figure out how to be a man with Cerebral Palsy within the dominant culture through the networks, communities, and cultures that we intentionally develop despite the shadow of institutionalization that for so long arrested the development of CP cultures. This raised my disability consciousness and helped me learn how to be a man with Cerebral Palsy. I suspect this is part of why Justin assures us that his proposal does not necessitate that "we abandon our pride in our unique disabled situations."

I do not know whether Justin intended to make repeated references to his pride in his Cerebral Palsy, but I am glad that he did because many theological considerations of disability ignore the existence of CP Pride. Taking CP pride as a non-negotiable starting point, however, ensures that Justin's theological project does not become a strained justification for the existence of folks with disabilities that dominant culture often demands of us to make them comfortable with our existence. Justin's unapologetic CP pride allows him to engage pressing problems that tend to preoccupy theological works on disability without confusing the nature of these problems. His Cerebral Palsy is primarily a source of pride rather than a social or theological problem.

In the lines that I quoted at the beginning of this foreword Justin acknowledges that his Cerebral Palsy is a struggle. Yet, he frames this struggle primarily within the larger social and political context of disability rights or liberation movements. Any readers unfamiliar with these movements will begin to learn the histories of this struggle from Justin's well-researched work. The social legacies of people with disabilities in the church in the United States are partially what necessitate Justin's invitation to the church in the first place. It is not the existence of disabilities themselves that necessitate this invitation. In the context of the legacies that Justin documents in this project, it is the larger Church rather than folks with disabilities that should, to invoke W. E. B. Dubois, consider how it feels to be a problem. I suspect that it is easier for some people, including many of the well-meaning theologians discussing disability today, to think of Cerebral Palsy as a struggle rather than the unexplained source of pride that it is for Justin. Yet, only ablism would demand an explanation for why Justin is proud of his Cerebral Palsy.

I would encourage readers to study the following pages closely and accept Justin's invitation to know him as a person who is proud of his Cerebral Palsy. Yet, in order to take this invitation seriously, one must accept the fact that one can be proud of one's

Cerebral Palsy as the uncompromising starting point for any engagement with not only Justin's proposal but, I would hope, any future theological discussions of disability.

Jeremy Schipper
Associate Professor of Hebrew Bible
Director of Graduate Studies, Department of Religion
Temple University

Acknowledgments

THERE ARE COUNTLESS PERSONS who deserve to be recognized within these acknowledgements. Without the tireless efforts of a great team of friends and colleagues, this journey never would have happened. For this, I am eternally grateful. First, I need to thank a wonderful group of people who served as my scribes throughout this process. To Margaret Elder, who was there at the very beginning, thank you for putting up with me when I didn't know my head from my feet with this project. To Robert Bishop and Brett Wells, my wonderful colleagues at the Missional Wisdom Foundation, thank you for being there as this project really began to take full shape and for helping me look at the same passages over and over to make sure we got the references exactly right. And, to David Schmersal, without whose tireless energy through the end of the writing process and the entirety of three edits this book never would have happened, thank you for always having honest and forthright opinions about the writing and a Monty Python quote ready for all occasions.

My sincerest, heartfelt thanks to Jane Elder, reference librarian at Bridwell Library at Perkins School of Theology, who was always there to read key parts of the draft whenever needed and helped me keep my sense of humor up and running at times when I felt hopelessly lost in the weeds. Also, thank you to all of the Bridwell staff for allowing Bridwell Library to be my writing and research home for the better part of almost five years. Thank you for letting me hang out at Bridwell even as I finished my work at Perkins nearly ten years ago.

I had help from a marvelous editorial team on all sides of this project. First, many thanks to Andrea Lingle at the Missional Wisdom Foundation, whose persistence in helping me make sure my argument was coherent at all points of this project was invaluable. Andrea's work in putting paragraphs in their right places and constantly encouraging me to write to my highest ability truly helped me use the prophetic voice I intended in this book. My sincerest thanks to Heather Carraher at Wipf & Stock for her help in typesetting the book on what was a tight schedule for publication. Finally, I owe an incalculable debt of gratitude to my editor at Wipf & Stock, Charlie Collier, for his friendship and support throughout this project, and his abundant willingness to take a phone call regarding even the tiniest question. I also cannot go without thanking all those who read early drafts of this manuscript as it was searching for a home, including Dr. Elaine Heath, Bishop Max Whitfield, Bishop Peggy Johnson, and Dr. Jeremy Schipper. To Jeremy, let me add an additional note of thanks for his wisdom, wonderful friendship, and a spectacular foreword.

I began dreaming about this project with encouragement from Dr. Larry Duggins and my colleagues at the Missional Wisdom Foundation. The Missional Wisdom Foundation is a fantastic place to work and has allowed me to take chances in ministry that no one else would. They also had the courage to hire somebody in a leadership role with a significant disability. For this, my family and I are eternally grateful, and I look forward to what adventures are around the bend.

Finally, I would like to thank my family. My wife, to whom this book is dedicated, is my best friend and greatest partner in ministry. To my parents, who always respected my bodily difference but never let me hide behind it or use it as an excuse for not doing my best, I say thank you. To my older brother Jeff, thank you for meeting me with love and encouragement from a very young age, letting me tag along with you and your friends, and knocking me around as all big brothers should do from time to time. To Jason, my twin brother, greatest ally, and eventual best friend, your steely-eyed determination that I would be where everyone else was is what allowed me to see that everything is possible with a little bit of creativity and a whole lot of courage. Your friendship and determination as you have faced your own struggles in recent years has brought us closer, and for this I am immensely grateful.

Introduction

EARLY IN MY MARRIAGE, my wife Lisa and I took a vacation to Fredericksburg, Texas, to spend a few days at one of our favorite bed-and-breakfasts. It was during a lunch date on one of those days that I came face to face with the un-reality that disability can often be for those who are able-bodied. We had just finished a delightful lunch and I was waiting by the door while Lisa went to get the manager so the door with the ramp could be unlocked (let's not even stop to think about the fact that the door with the ramp was at the back of the building and used so infrequently that it was locked). While waiting, I was engaged in conversation with a charmingly sweet older couple who were also vacationing in Fredericksburg from Philadelphia, Pennsylvania. The couple had obviously seen Lisa and me together because they asked me, "That woman you're here with, is that your sister?" When the word "sister" emerged with all the innocence and naivety of someone asking a genuine question, I felt like I was floating out of body, out of time—almost completely disconnected from the reality around me. When, after what felt like twenty minutes but was probably no more than a few seconds, I raised my left hand, smiled, and showed them my wedding ring, the look of dawning comprehension on their faces led me to believe that that charming couple from Pennsylvania was now engaged in a very similar out-of-body experience. Over the years, I have seen my wife referred to as my nurse, my sister, and my therapist; once, in a move that has me working on a sitcom pilot to this day, a nurse prepping me for surgery asked my wife, who is five years younger than I am, if she was my mother. I begin with these shocking and somewhat humorous mistakes only to tell you, my reader, that this is often the way in which my position as a disabled person is brought home.

I was raised in a profoundly loving home, with two brothers who were able-bodied and parents who were able-bodied. Their love and support allowed me every opportunity to excel in the largely able-bodied framework in which I lived. All of my friends—with the exception of a few whom I met every summer at the Texas Lions camp, a camp exclusively catering to children with disabilities—were able-bodied. What that created was a situation like the one I referenced at the beginning of this introduction. Most often, when someone confronted my disability, it was in a humorous situation of dislocation or within a medicalized context. Even in church, a place where I felt loved and accepted from childhood and every modification was made for me to participate and lead in my youth group, when my disability was theologically framed it was most often problematized or "super-ized" as some kind of gift or special blessing. Let me say again: I don't have any anger for those I grew up with or those who taught me within the church and within my life as a whole. I think it is my upbringing in a largely able-bodied framework that allows me to write this book today.

In what follows, I begin by tracing the origins and development of the disability civil rights movement from the opening of the twentieth century, beyond the passage of the Americans with Disabilities Act (ADA) in 1990, and into the early part of the twenty-first century. Readers might be surprised to learn, given my position as a highly-educated man with Cerebral Palsy, that until about five to seven years ago I was largely unaware that there was a disability civil rights movement and that often times this movement worked in concert with and enhanced the broader civil rights movement of the 1950s and 1960s.

Additionally, it is with some degree of sheepishness that I admit that before beginning my research I was largely unaware of the concept of the models of disability with which I deal in the opening pages. I hope as you read the first few chapters of this

work that you too, dear reader, will learn how my cultural fore-
bears struggled and fought for disability civil rights. I hope you
are greeted with the same sense of admiration and gratitude that
I have when you hear about those who engaged in sit-ins in city
halls to advocate for greater accessibility in public spaces. And I
hope that a discussion of the models of disability, and the ways
they encourage people like myself to find new and expansive ways
to conceive of their own reality, invites you, the reader, to discover
new ways of exploring your place in this larger world.

After the first section is complete, it is my desire to take you
on a journey through the relationship between people with disabilities and the church. We will examine the works of several of
the Western church's most prominent theologians down through
the ages, including St. Augustine and Karl Barth. I will show that
the church's lack of attention to doing theology in a way that allows
for an ever-shifting cultural and sociological context has led to a
situation in which many people with disabilities feel marginalized
and isolated, if not outright abused, by the church's approach to
their lives and embodiments. Again, I believe it is my location as a
clergyperson in the church with a deep love for its history, theology, and people that allows me to come at this task with a sincere
desire to facilitate conversations that lead to growth, change, and
empowerment for all of God's people regardless of their location
or circumstance. I wanted to write a book that encouraged the
person in the pew to think deeply about their own space and location within the church so that they could then develop a better
understanding for their friends, family, and fellow congregants
who experience any number of disabling embodiments. On the
way, I engaged theological concepts that were sometimes difficult
for me to grasp, concepts that often allowed me the privilege of
sitting with them for days and weeks until I was able to find new
levels of relevance and applicability to disability in our contemporary context.

There were times when I came to the theological study involved fully convinced I knew what I needed, only to have my
expectations and even my desires overturned again and again. At

moments, it felt like I drank one cup of coffee for every word I wrote. But whether the theology I was studying at that time was surprising, shocking, or downright elusive, unfailingly, when I finished engaging with a theologian, be they contemporary or ancient, I felt myself changed. As you begin to explore this material and encounter words, theologies, and concepts that may be new to you, or at least applied in a way that you have never explored them up until now, I hope and pray that you would let yourself be overwhelmed, delighted, and challenged and that this piece of writing would offer you an opportunity to begin to know things in a way that is more open, daring, and generous than perhaps you have ever experienced before.

The final section uses a new and deepening theological imagination to paint a picture of an intentional Christian community where the able-bodied and the disabled live, play, and do ministry together. As we encounter a day in the life of the Julian Way, I want you to begin to see yourself in that place, living and being in a community that is fully open and integrated to whatever experience or embodiment life might bring its way. It is this holy imagination that leads us beyond normalcy and towards variety and helps us encounter theologies that don't just work towards wholeness but rather invite us into experiencing the fullness of God's kingdom on earth in all its strangeness, diversity, and wonderful beauty.

I didn't write this book to win an argument or convince anyone that I am right about any particular issue. I wrote this book to introduce you to people you see every day, to welcome you into a world that you already inhabit but may have never fully experienced. As you read, may you experience disability and all its beauty, complexity, and struggle for all it's worth. If you can do that, I will know that I have done my job well.

PART I

Disability: Conceptions, Civil Rights, and Theology

Models of Disability

I WILL BEGIN THIS book by examining five distinct approaches to the study and understanding of disability, popularly called the "models of disability." The ones that we will look at in these opening pages are the medical model, the moral model, the social model, the limits model, and finally the cultural model. While the medical, moral, and social models are far and away most influential in helping us develop our latter twentieth- and early twenty-first-century approaches to disability, the limits and cultural models attempt to provide an innovative framework for helping us better understand the disability experience. I will begin our exploration of each model with a brief story or narrative vignette to help you, my reader, gain a slightly more first-hand perspective on the models of disability.

Medical Model

It's the summer of 2008, and my wife Lisa and I had been married exactly one week when we went to the mountains of New Mexico for a three-day honeymoon getaway. The mountain air was great, the feeling of being newly married was both invigorating and like a whole new adventure, and the time together was absolutely splendid. Upon checking out from the hotel, the desk clerk mentioned that she had seen us around the last several days and looking at my wife holding my bath chair before loading it into the car, she asked, "So, that guy you're with, are you his nurse or physical therapist?" I wish I could relate this story in the context of being a one-time-only humorous, isolated incident, or even, heck, an occasional occurrence would be nice. Unfortunately, I cannot count the number of times that my wife has been asked by strangers whether she is my physical therapist, my nurse, or my home care worker. The frequency of these situations during our nearly nine-year marriage only seems to underscore the level to which the general public largely and almost exclusively engages disability and the life of disabled people through the lens of a medical situation or circumstance. During my time speaking to local congregations and other church bodies regarding disability theology and the rights and dreams of people with disabilities, I am often surprised at how much amazement there is within my audiences when I point out that the medical model of disability is indeed only one way of understanding the disabled experience. Despite the seeming pervasiveness of the medical model, it is indeed one, just one, of many models or approaches to disability.

It would not be an exaggeration to say that the medical model is the overwhelmingly dominant mode of discourse surrounding disability in general society. The medical model, in its simplest form, locates disability within the body of an individual, most specifically in the malfunction of some specific part of the body or bodily process. In her book, *Disability and Christian Theology*, Deborah Creamer offers some indication of the ubiquity of the medical model when she suggests, "this model is closest to the commonsense idea that a disability is what someone has when his or her body or mind does not work properly."[1] This viewpoint on disability is so taken for granted within the general culture that it is no longer seen as one viewpoint or model among many, but a given fact. I contend that if one were to ask a hundred people on the street to give the easiest and most common definition of disability, it would invariably fall within the medical model.

1. Creamer, *Disability and Christian Theology*, 10.

The medical model, as it is now understood, did not begin to take hold in the United States and Europe until the end of the nineteenth and early twentieth centuries. Arguably, the medicalization of disability truly took root in the effort to denote difference in relation to a standard of normality. Such attitudes can be seen in the early twentieth century during what Sharon L. Snyder calls "eugenics-era legislation." For instance, the 1911 Chicago Ugly Law proclaimed: "any person who is diseased, maimed, mutilated or deformed in any way so as to be an unsightly or disgusting object is hereby prohibited from exposing himself to public view."[2] Lest one be tempted to think that such thinking is a relic from a bygone age, the forced institutionalization of many people with severe physical and intellectual disabilities was a fairly standard practice until the early 1970s.

This particular model actually exposes a thought process existent for centuries regarding disability. The physical flaws of persons with disabilities have even been used as metaphors for a whole host of societal ills. For instance, "whereas an ideal such as democracy signifies an abstracted notion of governmental and economic reform, de Baecque argues that the embodied caricature of a hunchbacked monarch overshadowed by a physically superior democratic citizen, for example, proves more powerful than any ideological argument."[3]

Although disability rights took a quantum leap forward with the passage of the Americans with Disabilities Act (ADA) on July 26, 1990, followed swiftly by the Individuals with Disabilities in Education Act (IDEA), which President George H.W. Bush signed into law on October 30, 1990, individuals and families that deal with disabilities are still living in a world where they confront the medical model of disability as the singular view almost from the beginning of life.

Gail Landsman explores the early exposure many mothers of young disabled children have to the medical model in her article, "Mothers and Models of Disability." Out of her study, Landsman

2. Snyder and Mitchell, *Cultural Locations of Disability*, 181–82.
3. Mitchell, *Narrative Prosthesis*, 27.

discovered that "in their encounters with a variety of early inter-vention service providers, mothers tend to experience the medical model in its rehabilitation variant."[4]

In this version of the medical model, the goal of therapy with children who are developmentally delayed is to move toward or approximate the norm in appearance and behavior. For example, the list of aims in a pediatric physical therapy text for early treat-ment of a child with Cerebral Palsy includes "[developing] normal postural reactions and postural tone . . . [counteracting] the devel-opment of abnormal postural reactions and of abnormal postural tone . . . [and preventing] the development of . . . deformities."[5] In this list of goals, we see the other side of the coin of the medical model. Where earlier we saw objectionable, outmoded laws such as the Chicago Ugly Law, now we see the more benign and gentle side of the medical model. The rehabilitation undertaken by many medical professionals regarding individuals with disabilities can truly have positive aims. Yet, the medical model still medicalizes disability to the point where the goal is to achieve "normality."

Social Model

A year and a half into our married life, my wife and I had saved for a large-scale honeymoon trip to Disney World. During the first day at Disney World, we were at the Hollywood Studios when my wife remembered that the Rockin' Roller Coaster was located there. Being a rollercoaster aficionado, Lisa knew we had to go. The thing that makes the Rockin' Roller Coaster different from other rides, along with its incredible speed and loud music, is that it is in an indoor roller coaster where the track is located in the floor of the building, which means that the ride actually launches from a point slightly below floor level, which means that my wife had to take me from my chair and bend down and with the help of other ride patrons get me positioned in the roller coaster seat.

4. Landsman, "Mothers and Models of Disability," 125.
5. Landsman, "Mothers and Models of Disability," 125.

While this is inconvenient, it is something I have basically been doing all of my life. My social-model real world experience truly began when getting out of the ride. First of all, I should say that the person operating and supervising the ride probably knew we were in for a rude shock, because they let us go around twice, which, as far as I know is unheard of at a ride at Disney World. At this point I should also add that Disney World as a company is largely renowned within their theme parks for paying special attention and taking exceptional care of children and families with a wide and complex range of disabilities. Part of the reason we wanted to go on our honeymoon there is that they had taken such good care of me as a small child. When I was a child, that excellent experience just sort of happened, so I was unaware of any preparatory work my parents had done in obtaining special disability access passes or any equivalent identification. So, imagine my surprise when, disembarking from the roller coaster—from below floor level, mind you—my wife and I had to essentially have me crawl out of the roller coaster car up onto the floor, and then crawl from the floor up into my chair, all while ride staff watched, unwilling or unable to help, all because we did not have the relevant disability identification. I should say that after we got the handicap access pass and diligently explained to other ride operators that we were not going to sue them if anything should happen, the rest of our vacation passed swimmingly. But on that day, in that moment, both because of the physical barriers located in the design of the roller coaster and because I did not have the proper park identification marking me as someone who had a socially acceptable disability, I was forced to experience the limitations and physical hardships of my disability to a degree that up until that point I never had before. When the pioneers of the social model talked about the barriers of the physical and social environment changing something from an impairment to a disability, this is precisely the type of experience to which they were pointing.

The social or minority group model of disability offers a viewpoint on disability that does not see disability as purely a medical phenomenon. Rather than viewing the world of disability through a medical lens, this framework proposes that an individual dealing with physical difficulties is an impaired individual. Disability, then, comes about when the impaired individual interacts with a social environment that imposes physical and societal barriers to their full participation in society and/or views their impairment in inherently negative terms. The social model was first developed in Britain through the work of sociologist Michael Oliver and others whose arguments were formalized in a 1976 statement of the Union of the Physically Impaired Against Segregation claiming that:

> It is society which disables physically impaired people. Disability is something imposed on top of our impairments by the way we are unnecessarily isolated and excluded from full participation in society. Disabled people are therefore an oppressed group in society. To understand this it is necessary to grasp the distinction between the physical impairment and the social situation called "disability" of people with such impairment. Thus, we define impairment as lacking all or part of a limb, or having a defective limb, organism or mechanism of the body and disability as the disadvantage or restriction of activity caused by a contemporary social organization which takes little or no account of people who have physical impairments and thus excludes them from participation in the mainstream of social activities. Physical disability is therefore a particular form of social oppression[6]

The above quotation demonstrates the goal of the social model—to move the disability conversation from one dealing with medical issues and a "normal versus different" dialectic towards a conversation that works for social and political action. The social model seeks to illustrate disability as an issue of civil rights and justice for all. A proponent of the social model would argue that nothing about impairment is inherently disabling. Only when an individual experiences the curative aspect of the medical model do they get caught up in a societal pressure towards normality. Hence, out

6. Union of the Physically Impaired, *Fundamental Principles*, http://disability-studies.leeds.ac.uk/files/library/UPIAS-fundamental-principles.pdf.

of this social framework disability advocates began protesting the use of physical therapy and curative techniques for the disabled.

Disability rights activists often point to greater visibility of impaired people and landmark legislation, such as the Americans with Disabilities Act, as proof that political action is effective. Moreover, social barriers, such as forced institutionalization and the aforementioned "ugly laws," have fallen by the wayside thanks to the social efforts of many impaired people. However, there are two distinct drawbacks to the social model of disability that have begun to emerge after closer scrutiny over the last fifteen to twenty years.

First, the social model is largely based around finding commonality between people with disabilities in order that they might fight for change and achieve large-scale civil rights victories. Yet, the task of finding a common disabled experience from which to start often proves next to impossible because of the sheer number and diversity of disabling conditions. In the article, "Models of Disablement, Universalism and the International Classification of Impairments, Disabilities and Handicaps," the author points to the fact that "not only are the social responses to different forms of mental and physical impairments vastly different, from the other direction, there is almost no commonality of experience, or feelings of solidarity, between people with diverse disabilities."[7] Thus, when one tries to develop a unified experience of disability, it often appears to be based on purely artificial constructs of unity that only address the most superficial aspects of the individual disabled experience.

The critique of artificial unity within the social model is hardly the only criticism. Possibly a more pointed, even damning, criticism centers on the neglect of the physical body within the social model framework. The social model focuses so intensely on the physical and societal barriers placed in front of physically and mentally impaired individuals that it almost wholly divorces itself from their physical reality. It either chooses to deny the important role of physical experience in personal development or selects to

7. Bickenbach et al., "Models of Disablement," 1181.

9

elevate suffering beyond the point of connection with any real, tangible experience.

"Contesting Representations of Disabled Children in Picture Books: Visibility, the Body and the Social Model of Disability" by Nicole Matthews tells the story of a young man who was involved in a project seeking to employ a wider range of disabled images in children's literature. He chose to write a story of Cinderella where the conflict resulted from the young heroine's incontinence. The editors of the project were uncomfortable with the issue of wetting being a dominant characterization of disabled life. To quote Matthews, "this discomfort with some dimensions of the behaviour of both disabled and non-disabled bodies reflects the social model's emphasis on impairment as a private, individual matter in contrast to the shared, political concerns about oppression and discrimination."[8] Critics of the social model argue that one cannot see a true description of disability without engaging with its physical consequences. Denying the physical aspect of disability is not only naïve, but dangerous. To divorce the physical body from the experience of personhood divides a person into an unhealthy, false dichotomy, and carries the potential of further objectifying persons with disabilities by denying voice to their physical experience. While the social model is necessary because of its call to action and pursuit of justice, critics have argued that it has swung so far from the medical model that it may have lost any sense of physical grounding in the day-to-day reality of disability.

Moral Model

In the spring of 2001, as a nineteen-year-old freshman in college, I was part of a group from the Wesley Foundation at West Texas A&M who were spending a week doing mission work with the Youth with a Mission (or YWAM) team in Chicago. This was the trip where I first began to discover two of my greatest joys in life: working and being in community with those in inner city or urban

8. Matthews, "Contesting Representations," 40.

neighborhoods, and the city of Chicago itself. This wonderful experience took a brief turn on a Sunday morning, however, after my group had attended worship at the Pentecostal church in downtown Chicago where we were staying for that week. The service had been great, and by and large all of the people we had met that Sunday had been nothing but delightful. I was enjoying the early spring air and sun out on the sidewalk in front of the church while my friends went down the street to take a look at a local landmark, when a man approached me who had apparently been in the same service that I had just attended. He walked up to me and asked if he could pray for me. At which point I told him, "Yes, I have a policy of never turning down prayer, if someone is willing to offer it. But before you begin, you should know that God and I have had many conversations and as of now, God is perfectly comfortable with me in a wheelchair and I am perfectly comfortable in the wheelchair." At which point the man reacted by saying words that I cannot repeat in the pages of this book, and calling me all sorts of names associated with sin, ingrate, etc. As my friends returned to my spot on the sidewalk, I exclaimed "You won't believe what just happened to me! A guy over there just cursed me out 'cause I didn't want to be healed!" Looking back on it now, over a decade and a half later, I was so bewildered by the whole experience that all I could do with my friends is laugh out loud at the utter absurdity of the whole episode. I had not the language then to know what I know now—that I had just been a victim, first-hand, of the moral model of disability. That person's image of God, and of me as a disabled person, was so tied into my disability being a blemish or an evil or a problem to be solved that when I refused prayer on his grounds and refused to see myself in his all-too-narrow religious framework, I think that blew his mind. I would come to learn later that my experience was not nearly as rare as perhaps I would have wished. Hence, the moral model of disability.

As prominent as the medical and social models have proven to be, alternative models also need to be addressed when one examines the larger conversation around disability in society today. The two most notable alternatives are the moral model and the limits model, both of which have beneficial and non-beneficial aspects. The moral model of disability most frequently finds a home in institutions of faith and tends to present similar issues to those found within the medical model. In fact, most people who find themselves addressing disability using aspects of the moral model do not even know they are using a particular framework within which to think and talk about disability because many of the assumptions born out of the moral model have penetrated many religious spheres within general society.

So, what do I mean when I mention a moral model of disability? In *Vulnerable Communion,* Thomas E. Reynolds contends that there are two predominant strands of the moral model. First is the denigrating view of disability. Reynolds explains that "here, disabled bodies are portrayed as less than whole, suffering from an incompleteness or lack of some significant, creaturely wholeness that is perceived as sacred and reflective of God's nature and perfection."[9] There are countless stories of healing in the New Testament that function within this pattern, such as the paralytic lowered through a roof in Mark 2:1–12 and the woman with the issue of blood in Matthew 9:20–22. The healings in both of these stories have been traditionally interpreted as a return to wholeness from a broken state. There are numerous other texts in the New Testament that tell a similar story and seem to imply that a person's disability is directly related to sin. Additionally, the ancient Hebrew code of law is laced with references to people with physical or mental abnormalities as unclean. This often leads us to view persons with disabilities as somehow beyond the grace of God, even if it is only for a short time. One might be forgiven for thinking that the denigration of disability is largely a matter for ancient times, but sadly, this is not the case. I, myself, have been in situations where students I discipled in my work as a United Methodist clergyperson were insistent about praying for my healing. Some even actively tried to heal me. For the purposes of complete honesty, I will admit there were times that I bought into the notion of being healed, even with some enthusiasm. I think this speaks

9. Reynolds, *Vulnerable Communion,* 36.

to the prevalence of the moral model's viewpoint and how easily someone with a physical impairment can get caught up in the notion of restorative healing. I was shocked at the number of times a student would come to me with issues and allow me to disciple them, while still conceiving of my disability as a lack or blemish within my own spirituality.

The denigration of disabilities is not the only way the moral model is used. Reynolds calls the second part of the moral model the "trivialization of disability." There are two main ways that disability is trivialized. First, persons with disabilities act as charity cases through which the nondisabled can demonstrate their piety and goodness by working to alleviate suffering.[10] Reynolds, along with many other disability advocates quoted in this book, points out that entire service systems and programs, like Jerry's Kids, are founded on this principle. This is a classic example of the road to hell being paved with good intentions. Whatever the good intentions might be, this way of thinking reduces disabled individuals to passive presences who are acted upon without taking an active role in their own identity and care. This can have the unintended consequence of perpetuating stereotypes of helplessness and neediness rather than actively helping and engaging with a particular physical or mental issue.

Second, the moral model also promotes the virtuous suffering argument. This argument states that individuals with disabilities are imbued with a special holiness and divine understanding simply because they deal with a disability. I have often heard friends say things such as, "Your situation puts all of my issues in perspective." I have a friend with Crohn's disease and colitis who has told me that very thing. This only served in my mind to underscore the point that it is not just "completely" nondisabled people that feel this way, but even individuals who are perceived to be somehow "less disabled" than I am.

The attachment of virtue to disability is dangerous in whatever form it takes. There are even those who say that because I am strong, God gave me disabilities because God knew I could

10. Reynolds, *Vulnerable Communion*, 38–41.

handle it. The virtuous suffering argument is ridiculous because it presumes an erroneous belief about God. Such a belief holds that God would distribute a disproportionate amount of hardship into somebody's life because that person is uniquely virtuous or has exceptional inner strength of character; therefore the suffering seems intended to balance the cosmic or cosmological scales. The virtuous suffering argument also reduces human capacity to respond to suffering in the fullness of free will or agency. Disabled individuals are not given an opportunity to express a full range of emotions and are placed in a super-moral box from which it is virtually impossible to escape. To put it another way, as a disabled person and a United Methodist pastor, I consider myself to be a genuinely compassionate person. However, this has no inherent link to my disability. I still occasionally suffer from the bad moods and general stupidity that all human beings experience. I do acknowledge the unique life lessons I have been taught as a disabled male that many nondisabled persons never experience, at least not at my age. But these lessons are not internalized merely because I am disabled. No matter a person's situation, these opportunities must be recognized for what they are in the moment in order to gain meaning and learn from them in a helpful manner.

Limits Model

People often ask me questions like, what do I find most challenging about my physical disability. I find invariably that those people want me to say something like "never having the sensation of running while playing sports" or wanting me to reflect on something I miss in my daily life because I am physically incapable of experiencing it due to my Cerebral Palsy. Without fail, people who ask that and similar questions want me to reflect on some meta or all-encompassing hardship related to disability. I often find however that the small stuff presents the greatest challenge: whether it is the times when my wife and I are out in public and, despite every indication that a restaurant or bus stop is accessible, the doors are too narrow and the curb cuts are all but non-existent, or the times when, because of the way I sit, an urge to use the restroom sneaks up on me and I am unable to answer nature's call quite fast enough. These are the times I am challenged by disability. And this is precisely what theologian and activist Deborah Beth Creamer would call "the Limits Model of Disability" because I am most effectively or truly disabled when encountering those aspects that most clearly cause me to experience the limiting effects of my disability. Creamer explains in her book *Disability Theology* that the limits model attempts to remove disability from the realm of solid category as seen in the social model and medical model. Where the medical model works from a purely physical construct and the social model defines disability as a social and civil rights driven issue, Creamer proposes that we must acknowledge both the physical and social dimensions of disability through an examination of human limits. The basic premise of the model is that all humans have limits, and we all attempt to deny that we are limited creatures. Within the disabled context, the limits model serves to offer a framework for people to understand their disability through their day-to-day experiences. For example, there are days when the cold weather impacts the arthritis in my hips. Creamer would say on those days I feel more disabled than on days when I do not feel the consequences of arthritic hips. Creamer proposes that disability is not always an "are" or "are not" but also a "when," "where," or "how."[11]

While I applaud this model for its attempt to address both medical and social aspects of disability in addition to the lived experience of disability, it also has its shortfalls. First among these criticisms is the fluidity argument. This model puts so much stock into the fluid situation of disability that it does not adequately take into account, in my opinion, the degree to which the physical and social consequences of disability are operative within the life of a disabled person, regardless of what they feel or do not feel on a given day. In addition, I do not feel the model goes far enough in its description of disability, primarily because it does not square enough with my experience of disability. There are times that I

11. Creamer, *Disability and Christian Theology*, 19.

deal with medical and health complications that are extremely real, and then there are moments where, although I feel medically well, the physical barriers to mobility as well as the latent social stigma or anxiety that often accompany disability, are very real and ever present. But, whether my primary mode of engaging my disability experience on a given day is medical or social, my disability is always there. Further, the limits model can easily fall into the reductive trap of "everyone is disabled." As long as an argument of limits still fails to engage the larger culture in conversation about the marginalization of disabled people, it does not matter how much you point out the limits every person encounters. Thus, if everyone is disabled and disability acts as a fluid definer, then the limits model upholds the power of those who can consistently pass as "abled" in the culture without promoting the power of persons with disabilities. All the models that we have discussed—medical, moral, social, and limits—try in some way, shape, or form to give a cultural voice to the experience of being disabled. Yet, these models suffer from significant shortfalls that prevent them from integrating disabled individuals fully into a common experience of God-given humanity.

Cultural Model

In the summer of 2013, I attended for the first time the Summer Institute for Theology and Disability, a yearly gathering of theologians, activists, and scholars interested in and working with issues of disability and religion. It was at this summer conference that I had the privilege of being part of a situation that, in my experience, was almost completely unprecedented: there were at least seven people with Cerebral Palsy around one table at one time. You must understand that in my childhood and during my adolescence, this type of phenomenon only occurred during my yearly trip to the Texas hill country for Texas Lions camp, a camp for children with disabilities. This was probably the first time in my adult life when I had seen more than two or three people with Cerebral Palsy, let alone other disabilities, in one space at one time. There was a

45-minute period at the beginning of that day's conference festivities where the table participants simply had an opportunity to get to know one another. The conversation that occurred during that 45 minutes was astounding in its openness, its depth, and its humor and sarcasm. The nine people around that table talked in startlingly clear terms about the medical and physical issues that come with their disability, as well as the social and legal barriers that can also come with disability. The conversation flowed so effortlessly through all aspects of disability that it was truly a sight to behold. I can say without exaggeration that it was that three-day conference and in large part my experience around that table that fully convinced me to devote my life to disability issues in the church. And that table conversation also is the greatest example of the cultural model of disability I have ever seen, because during those 45 minutes disability was not a one-dimensional medical or social or moral experience. Those nine voices came with a multitude of realities about what disabilities meant to them. Nobody was cheated, nobody's experience was given priority. Everyone's experience was real, true, and helped inform the identity of the larger group. In that conversation around that table on that day, were a people with a unique cultural viewpoint. This is, in a nutshell, the cultural model of disability, a model that takes into account both the medical reality and the social reality of disability, and says we only have a fully informed disability experience when every factor is allowed to stand and be in conversation with everything else.

The history of the perception of disability has led, whether intentionally or unintentionally, to the adoption by the larger general culture of a split in the way persons are perceived on a scale of disability. Author and sociologist Robert McRuer describes this in his article "Disability Nationalism in Crip Times" as an "able-bodied–disabled binary." McRuer uses the work of other sociologists like Deborah Stone to point out that this binary is a largely Western phenomenon tied to the emergence of capitalism as the dominant economic and philosophical system. As the Industrial Revolution first began to grow and take hold in the West, society moved away from a largely agrarian identity in which people had to innately care for one another to survive. In the context of an agrarian society, disability was largely a communal or family matter, so, although the degree of care varied, care was always or most often available. However, as systems became more dependent on skilled labor those with disabilities were marked as useless and in need of categorization to differentiate between those who could work and those who needed assistance. Although this binary approach took hold slowly at first, McRuer and others point out that eventually the dominant culture normalized its own dominance until able-bodied versus disabled becomes the status quo instead of an artificially created reality. One can see the development of the models discussed in the prior sections as a natural outgrowth of this cultural shift.[12]

Individuals outside the disabled community do not often realize that an able/disabled binary exists. Within this binary is a kind of caste system drawn from state-based help systems such as Medicare, Medicaid, and Social Security. These systems often require strict definitions or frameworks to determine the severity of one's disability to evaluate their eligibility for government assistance. This, along with a number of other factors, can make it difficult for the disabled community to come together without bringing out biases and resentments based on a hierarchy of disability.

The cultural model offers an alternative linguistic lens that seeks to deconstruct the power of the able/disabled binary by utilizing the terminology of disabled/nondisabled. Schipper and Junior explain that in the cultural model, "the term 'nondisabled' may not describe an objective biological difference from persons with disabilities," reflecting instead the "cultural expectations for how frequently we might encounter a particular trait in a person of a particular age."[13] Thus, nondisabled "is not an objective description of normalcy"; rather, "cultural notions of nondisability and disability work together to shape and reinforce cultural

12. McRuer, "Disability Nationalism," 167.
13. Junior and Schipper, "Disability Studies and the Bible," 24.

understandings of normalcy.[14] Hence, the distinction of disabled/ nondisabled sets the cultural model apart and offers a useful and constructive alternative for a theology seeking to break down the able/disabled binary.

In response to the shortcomings of the models previously discussed, I propose an examination of the cultural model of disability as a guiding paradigm for this conversation between disability, society, and theology. The cultural model of disability seeks to create a full view of disability that more realistically accounts for the lived reality of physical impairment than the limits model. In his work as an Old Testament scholar and his experience as a man living with the daily reality of Cerebral Palsy, Jeremy Schipper describes the uniqueness of the cultural model perspective as compared to the social model of disability in his article "Mosaic Disability and Identity in Exodus 4:10; 6:12, 30." He writes, "Unlike the social model, the cultural model does not simply aim to isolate and remove social barriers for persons with disabilities, but it investigates how 'disability' as a conceptual category informs social or cultural worldviews and plays an integral part in social and cultural organization."[15]

Conclusion: Why the Cultural Model Is an Ideal Beginning for an Intentional Christian Community in the Disability Context.

At its core, the cultural model seeks to incorporate the complex individual, social, and cultural experiences that make up life with a disability. In their book *Cultural Location of Disability,* disability theorists David T. Mitchell and Sharon L. Snyder write, "This insight shifts disability from either a medical pathology or signifier of social discrimination into a source of embodied revelation."[16] Although Snyder and Mitchell were not speaking about a spiritual

14. Junior and Schipper, "Disability Studies and the Bible," 24.
15. Junior and Schipper, "Mosaic Disability and Identity," 432.
16. Snyder and Mitchell, *Cultural Locations of Disability,* 8.

or religious situation, I believe the statement they make here has dramatic spiritual consequences. The cultural model gives persons with disabilities the opportunity to interact in the larger Christian community where their disability serves no special purpose beyond being a further proof of the diversity of God's Kingdom and the embodiment of God's good creation. This "embodied revelation" truly begins to take form in God's not-yet-but-already-here Kingdom. Because the cultural model of disability does not emphasize one part of the disabled experience over another, it allows for a greater depth of conversation between people with a widely varying number of disabilities. Ultimately, this is our hope and dream for an intentional Christian community with disabled families.

Sadly, the church has done little to nothing to meet the disabled culture on its own terms. As stated above, for generations the majority of the church's engagement with disability has been largely focused around the healing or remediation of disability. As people of God, we rarely take note of those passages of Scripture that show disability in a different light.

While looking at different conceptions or ways of handling disability in the Old Testament, J. Blake Couey points out that unlike Isaiah and other Old Testament texts that refer to a level road or other mobility aids that might help the disabled, Jeremiah 31:8–9 is unique because the road is leveled specifically for the benefit of those with the disability.[17] Ultimately, I desire a level-road experience to take place in the Church. I believe a community where the nondisabled and disabled come together and learn in mutuality can be that sort of level-road experience.

I utilize the cultural model of disability because I believe it is the most effective way for nondisabled and disabled alike to truly engage on a level playing field. Hence, I have chosen to use the cultural model as the framework from which we will develop an intentional Christian community for families with disabilities. We believe that every perspective an individual brings into a community is unique and offers an added dimension of richness to the

17. Couey, "Disabled Body Politic," 106.

relationships within that community. This is especially true as it relates to the disabled culture. We will end this book by taking a narrative journey into The Julian Way that Lisa and I want to begin, so that we might be able to envision what daily life in an intentional Christian community based around the cultural model of disability might look like. As, in later chapters, we move into a closer examination of the church and its relationship to disability through theology, we will be looking at some of the preeminent thinkers in the history of Christian theology. In order to illustrate the implications their ideas may have for a theology of disability, we will consider what effects they may have in the lives of some of the characters we will meet more fully in the narrative section of the book. The community that will emerge from the work of the Julian Way is inspired, in part, by the vision of the Church offered in Acts 2:44–45 in which "all the believers were together and had everything in common. They sold property and possessions to give to anyone who had need." Only the power of the Kingdom of God can bring both the disabled and nondisabled to one holy table as a community of God's peace. This can only happen when we begin the conversation with language that embodies the fullness of all that God has created us to be. The cultural model is this beginning point.

2

Disability Civil Rights and the ADA

AT THIS POINT, IT is appropriate to look at what has come to be the most significant moment in the history of disability in the United States of America: the formation and passage of the Americans with Disabilities Act (ADA). In this section, I will offer a brief glance at the forces that led up to the ADA, both culturally and with regards to US domestic policy. Before beginning in earnest, please allow latitude for one small disclaimer: the movements and processes culminating in the ADA involve dozens of groups and hundreds of thousands of significant persons. It is not my intention to give an exhaustive history of every corner of the movement. I will leave someone or some group out. Please know that this omission is not intentional.

This section of the project has been both the most inspiring and exhausting endeavor to date. As a person with Cerebral Palsy (CP), I owe an incalculable debt of gratitude to all of those who fought for civil rights either through legislation or nonviolent protest. Hopefully what follows will do those brave people justice.

Preamble and Path Toward the ADA

The journey toward the ADA, culminating on July 26, 1990, began nearly forty years beforehand in the 1950s under President

Eisenhower. In the article, "A Historical Preface to the Americans with Disabilities Act," Edward Berkowitz points out in the 1950s:

> Policy makers located in the newly created Department of Health, Education, and Welfare (HEW) concentrated on two core projects . . . The first project concerned the expansion of the social security program, which had emerged as the nation's largest and most expensive social welfare program in 1951 . . . The second project involved the expansion of federal grants to the states to assist people with disabilities in finding jobs.[1]

Both of these programs were attempts by the United States government to address the visibility of individuals with disabilities in American society. Several disability sociologists and historians have noted that the focus on rehabilitation had much to do with the government's desire to move away from a Depression-era welfare state and toward an America that promoted independence for its disabled citizens.

The disabled community would later be formed in the cradle of civil rights known as the 1960s. Many young disabled Americans began to use the spirit of the times to advocate on their own behalf for the same civil rights and freedoms that were quickly spreading throughout the United States. In *Equality of Opportunity*, Jonathan Young writes:

> In the 1960s, the independent living movement gained momentum predominantly through the influence of college students. In 1962, for example, four students with disabilities at the University of Illinois at Champaign-Urbana helped start the movement by leaving an isolated facility to reside near campus in a home modified for accessibility and gain increased control over their own lives. A similar and more visible effort took place the same year, when Ed Roberts, who was paralyzed from polio, entered the University of California at Berkeley. The school housed him in the third floor of Cowell

---

1. Berkowitz, "Historical Preface," 96–119.

Hospital, where he was aided by friends and attendants with eating and dressing. Roberts thrived. He earned not only his undergraduate degree, but also a master's degree in political science.[2]

For a while, it seemed as though the emerging disability community would ride the wave of 1960s-era social change to new heights of recognition and freedom within the broader American culture. Unfortunately, this progress was briefly, if not dramatically, interrupted by a cultural backlash against the liberal social welfare climate of the 1960s exemplified by the rise of the conservative silent majority in the United States, which was epitomized by the election of President Richard Nixon in 1968.

The disability community still enjoyed the victory that came with the Architectural Barriers Act of 1968, a federal law mandating accessibility in all buildings owned by housing or administrated by the United States Government. Progress was slow, but not altogether stagnant thanks in large part to a Congress that was still dedicated to some degree of social change through federal policy. The forerunner to the modern ADA emerged in 1973 through the Rehabilitation Act. Known as "Section 500" this Act guaranteed certain civil rights for persons with disabilities on a level that had not previously been seen.

In *Equality of Opportunity*, Young writes:

> under section 503, parties contracting with the United States were required to use affirmative action to employ qualified persons with disabilities . . . Section 504 stated: "No otherwise qualified handicapped individual in the United States . . . shall, solely by reason of his handicap, be excluded from the participation in, be denied the benefits of, or be subjected to discrimination under any program or activity receiving Federal finance assistance."[3]

Although Congress passed the Rehabilitation Act and Section 500 provisions in September 1973, the actual implementation and

2. Young, *Equality of Opportunity*, 22.
3. Young, *Equality of Opportunity*, 13.

drafting of the regulations, which was the responsibility of HEW (Department of Health, Education and Welfare), became another unfortunate victim of the Watergate situation swirling around President Nixon. Although President Ford, who became president after Nixon's resignation, supported the drafting of regulations, HEW again failed to act in a timely fashion. Ultimately, the regulations would be stalled and tied up in red tape by three successive presidential administrations. As one might expect, such a bureaucratic nightmare began to galvanize the disability community.

Eventually, Georgetown's Institute for Public Interest Representation (INSPIRE) helped file suit against the federal government, demanding it bring forward actual regulations. At the same time, a group of disabled activists protested the slow movements of the federal government by occupying the office of the Secretary of HEW. After some time, the United States District Court for the District of Columbia ordered Secretary Mathews of HEW to bring forward regulations. Although this occurred in 1976, formal intent to bring forward regulations was not settled until almost a full year later.[4] Throughout the rest of the 1970s and into the early 80s, Section 504 and 503 became known as "The Civil Rights Legislation for the Handicapped."

The ordeal over the implementation of the regulations showed the disability community's potential as a civil rights lobbying group. This led to activists such as Paul Marchand and others to form the Consortium of Citizens with Developmental Disabilities (later shortened to CCDD) in 1975. CCDD's main function was to serve as an umbrella organization for many disability rights groups. Under their leadership and aggressive lobbying tactics, Congress and the federal government continued to pay ever more attention to the disabled community. CCDD was integral in the passage of such legislation as The Education for all Handicapped Children Act of 1975. Eventually, however, infighting among the CCDD's many member organizations led to its implosion.[5]

4. Young, *Equality of Opportunity,* 15.
5. Young, *Equality of Opportunity,* 26.

CCDD left a legacy of activism and change that would be carried forward by the most unlikely group imaginable: The National Council on the Handicapped (NCH). Although the NCH (later NCD) had been around since the early 1970s, its efforts, historically, could be described as sluggish at worst and symbolic at best. It took the ascension of Ronald Reagan to the presidency to shake the NCD from its slumber. In an effort to trim government spending and create a more tightly controlled federal system, Reagan disbanded the board as it was constituted in 1982 and appointed all new members. According to Young, he appointed Joe Dusenbury, formally the head of South Carolina Vocational Rehabilitation Services, as the head of the board.

If President Reagan's intention was to create an NCD through which the administration could dominate disability and social policy, the actions of Dusenbury, along with Vice Chairman Justin Dart and Sandra Parrino had the absolute opposite effect. The NCD created an ambitious report on the state of disability called *National Policy on Disability*. The scope of this report was nationwide and allowed Justin Dart's trademark style of grassroots coordination and face-to-face conversation to first emerge onto the national disability policy landscape. Although the report was a masterful combination of research and firsthand accounts, it would eventually cost Dusenbury the chairmanship of the committee because many Reagan administration officials were not happy with the tone or implications of the report. After it was issued, Dusenbury was removed under the pretext of rotating the chairmanship of the committee yearly. He was replaced by Vice Chairman Sandra Parrino, who went on to do extraordinary work during her chairmanship of four years. While all this was taking place inside the NCD, Vice President Bush was put in charge of a committee for deregulation. The job of Vice President Bush and others on this committee was to examine federal social policy and see what could be removed or stripped away in order to allow the Reagan budget office to trim federal expenditure.[6]

6. Young, *Equality of Opportunity*, 51.

Ironically, as with most things regarding disability policy in the Reagan administration, it did not work out quite as they had foreseen. Vice President Bush, instead of trimming disability legislation and other social programs, consistently advocated for increased rights for disabled individuals. Meanwhile, over at the NCD, Chairman Parrino and the rest of the committee were contemplating an ambitious report during their 1985 meeting that would build on and strengthen the recommendations in the 1983 report. This would eventually evolve into the report entitled *Toward Independence*. Committee members Lex Frieden and Robert Burgdorf led the charge in the construction and writing of this report.

The NCD eventually settled on ten topics: "equal opportunity laws, employment, disincentives to work under Social Security laws, prevention of disabilities, transportation, housing, community-based services for independent living, educating children with disabilities, personal assistant services, and coordination of disability policy and programs."[7] Within *Toward Independence*, we see the first real call for nationwide disability civil rights legislation. To put it another way, *Toward Independence* is the ground in which the seeds of the ADA were planted. It would take almost four years and several iterations before ADA reached final form, but in *Toward Independence*, we were firmly on that road. It should be noted that, just as with the 1983 report, White House officials were reluctant to get behind the publication of *Toward Independence*. Administration official Bob Sweet referred to the 1985 report as "so liberal, Ted Kennedy wouldn't produce it."[8]

After *Toward Independence* was produced and circulated among the disability community in 1986, momentum began to grow for a comprehensive piece of legislation that would do for disabled persons what the Civil Rights Act of 1964 accomplished for African Americans. Some within NCD even drafted a version of the ADA as early as 1986 knowing that the proposal would most likely not see the light of day. However, it was there when

7. Young, *Equality of Opportunity*, 55.
8. Young, *Equality of Opportunity*, 57.

the time did come. By 1988, the time had come. The confluence of a Congress with a significantly powerful Democratic presence, a growing disability rights movement, and an election year featuring a race between Michael Dukakis and Vice President George Bush, two men with superior records calling for greater disability rights, made the time appropriate to introduce the ADA into the legislative process.[9]

In 1988, in the midst of a presidential election contest in which the ADA would play a vital role, the Senate Subcommittee on the Handicapped began hearings on the ADA bill drafted earlier that year. The hearings were not intended to create the ADA in its final form, but merely to get disability rights into the national dialogue. In fact, both Senator Tom Harkin (D-IA), Chairman of the Subcommittee on the Handicapped, and Senator Lowell P. Weicker, Jr. (R-CT), one of the ADA's initial sponsors, pointed out that the 1988 hearings were not going to produce a final product.

The hearings, however, did produce moving testimony of the struggles of people with disabilities in America. For example, people like Mary Linden, who inaugurated the first panel, described growing up as a child with a disability due to doctors' surgical errors. Linden pointed out that she did not learn to write until after graduating from a disabled high school in 1951, and then only because she taught herself. Despite graduation from high school, Ms. Linden was unable to attend a four-year university because of inaccessible public transportation. She concluded her testimony by asking the Senate to pass this bill so that generations after her did not have to suffer like she did and so that disabled Americans could obtain "the most precious thing in the world, a paying job."[10]

Twelve-year-old Jade Calegory testified to the enormous benefit he received from the Education for all Handicapped Children Act because it allowed him to go to a public school with the rest of his friends and be in a normal setting.

There were stories about individuals who wanted to engage in the political process, but while trying to visit a campaign office,

9. Young, *Equality of Opportunity*, 92.

10. Young, *Equality of Opportunity*, 93.

couldn't find a handicapped parking spot wide enough to use their van lift. Another woman told a story of her struggle to find a job after being diagnosed with AIDS and HIV and suffering a stroke.

The testimony gave depth and variety to the 1988 hearings and helped paint a broad picture of discrimination that would set the stage for the ADA to reemerge and move towards final passage in 1989. It must be pointed out that one of the most powerful presences at both the 1988 and 1989 hearings was that of Justin Dart. In preparation for the fight over ADA, Dart once again went around the country using his trademark face-to-face style to collect discrimination diaries from hundreds of thousands of disabled citizens. These diaries told story after story of compelling testimony of discrimination.

With the election of Vice President George Bush to the presidency in 1988, it became clear that disability rights legislation would pass in some form under President Bush's leadership, so 1988–89 was the year to make the final push toward a workable law. To that end, Congress once again held hearings beginning with the introduction of the bill in May 1989. As in 1988, there was once again compelling testimony of those dealing with disabilities. As Congress turned to the ADA, this time with serious intent of passing a law, some notable sources of opposition and counter-argument began to emerge.

Overcoming Obstacles

The American Public Transportation Association (APTA), the main lobbying and trade organization for the public transit industry, had long been a source of frustration and deep discontent for the civil rights wing of the disability community because of their overwhelming opposition to equipping bus routes with lift-enabled buses. As the 1989 deliberations were in process, the disabled community protested APTA in many creative ways. Just to name a few, at the 1989 APTA convention they barred the entrance to the convention center, individuals in wheelchairs would crawl up bus steps and handcuff themselves to steering columns in cities such as

Denver, Houston, and other major transit centers, or, sometimes, protestors would literally lie down in front of fully loaded buses to prevent them from moving. Protests like these, along with the actions of Senators like Tom Harkin and Ted Kennedy and Representative Tony Coelho, eventually caused APTA to largely concede that ultimately equipping fixed-route buses with lifts was a cheaper alternative to solely offering para-transit services.[11]

Opposition from trade organizations like APTA is understandable to some degree or another. There was also understandable reservation from many legislators due to the cost of enacting a law that would require such broad and sweeping change. The economic effects of the ADA would emerge and re-emerge in both Senate hearings and in the House.

In fact, economics would be one of the most difficult hurdles for the ADA to overcome. What made this more challenging, ironically, was the ADA's very early alignment with previous civil rights legislation. During the 1989 hearings, the conversations between advocates within the government and senators reviewing the legislation threw the divide between civil rights legislation and its economic consequences into sharp relief. In an exchange within the Congressional hearings, we repeatedly hear the Acting Assistant Attorney General in the United States Department of Justice Civil Rights Division, Jim Turner, on the verge of defending the ADA and the changes it would require in order to point out its civil rights benefits. Again and again, Congressman Jim Olin (D-VA) interrupts the Acting Attorney General with the question of cost. "In unfinished statements such as these—and not in the content of the legislation alone—the contradictions between universal equality and the market took form."[12] Author Carol J. Greenhouse is making a larger point when she says this by trying to demonstrate that in a market-driven system, such as the United States, it is very hard to achieve sweeping civil and human rights change because the specter of economic cost will haunt any legislation that is produced.

11. Young, *Equality of Opportunity*, 124.
12. Greenhouse, "Ethnography and Democracy," 197.

I will conclude this chapter by examining something that has been an ongoing struggle for me throughout writing this book and since I began to study and investigate the disabilities civil rights movement and the passage of the ADA—that is, the relationship of the ADA to and with religious institutions within the United States. I will also offer a brief look at the progress of the Americans with Disabilities Act since its passage in 1990.

Before we move on, however, I would like to take a few moments of personal reflection around the long journey that led to the Americans with Disabilities Act. During the latter stages of preparation for publication, I had the privilege of working with a marvelous editor named Andrea Lingle. Andrea put paragraphs in the right places, moved thoughts around so they flowed better, and generally helped make this book a much more cohesive and understandable endeavor. As we came to placing finishing touches on the historical section of this project, Andrea politely and persistently encouraged me to include my own narrative among the historical and socio-political examination offered within these pages. I wrestled with and thought about this for several weeks, and I think I can legitimately say, looking back at it now, that growing up, this did not feel like my history. It was not withheld from me by any means; I just grew up in an entirely able-bodied environment. I have very vivid memories of that day in late-July 1990, when President Bush signed the Americans with Disabilities Act. I remember my mother saying "this is important for you. You are going to want to remember this" as we watched coverage of the signing on the evening news. But I did not grow up being aware of people lying down in front of buses to force the transportation industry to listen, or knowing about the numbers of people who testified during hearings about their inability to get a decent public education in the 1950s and 1960s. It's only been within the last three plus years since I have begun researching this book that these people's stories have become my story. People like Ed Roberts and his fellow disabled classmates who enrolled at Cal Berkley to break down educational barriers are now heroes of mine. I will emulate Justin Dart and his personable one-on-one style of advocacy for the rest of my natural days. Over the past several years, since my wife and I have been engaging in disability advocacy I have become fond of saying that the American with Disabilities Act is the floor, not the ceiling—that is, where conversation should begin, not end. It's because of the work done by the individuals highlighted in the preceding pages that I feel that way.

The Americans with Disabilities Act was and remains the piece of United States legislation that has had the greatest impact on my life, and its ever-changing and ever-evolving form and future continues to have consequences for me and every other disabled person in the United States. It would perhaps not be an exaggeration to say that along with my faith as a Christian the Americans with Disabilities Act is the single thing that allows me to engage life as fully as I do on a daily basis. I have witnessed, however, the unfortunate tension between the desire of religious institutions to be loving, kind, and inclusive of as many persons as possible and the messy, oftentimes less-than hospitable realpolitik nature that comes with being a religious institution.

Having grown up in the 1990s during and after the passage of the ADA, I have known for a number of years that religious communities were among the first to ask for and receive exemptions from the ADA from the federal government. I think I first became aware of this fact as a political reality sometime during my college years. I had assumed that this was due largely to the prohibitive cost of modifying and adapting many places of worship that had been around for decades. Although constant modification was and is a significant part of the resistance, the 1989 ADA hearings gave rise to a far more insidious reason for religious institutions opting out.

Many in the religious community felt that the Americans with Disabilities Act was an opportunity for the gay and lesbian community to assault the religious community's right to freedom of religion. As William Ball, representative of the Association of Christian Schools International, argued, "The ADA . . . would be too costly, might force schools to hire drug/alcohol abusers or homosexuals, and threatened the constitutional separation of church and state."[13] As much as I understand and defend the right for religious self-determination and freedom, especially as a clergy of the United Methodist Church, I can't help but feel that the religious exemption and the debate over the connection between ADA and HIV/AIDS is a stain on the church and the Congress alike, because it essentially said that in order to avoid a group we fear, we will avoid embracing another group entirely. Unfortunately, as we will see shortly, the church's exemption will come up again and again even to the present day.

Even though the ADA passed the Senate with flying colors and President Bush promised to sign the bill when it passed the House, challenges still remained. There is one more legislative challenge I would like to make note of. Evidence of the tie between the ADA and HIV/AIDS was brought into clear view with the proposal of the Chapman Amendment. Even though the ADA had always intended to cover HIV/AIDS and a large statement against HIV/AIDS discrimination had been made in the Fair Housing Amendments Act of 1988, Congressman Jim Chapman (D-TX) proposed an amendment that would ban individuals with contagious diseases from working in food handling positions within the restaurant industry. There was a great deal of consternation at this amendment from Senators and physicians who pointed out that there was no substantial, provable link between HIV and incidental contact with food or beverage. As Congressman Hamilton Fish put it, "The Congress cannot enshrine ignorance and prejudice in the law." Despite support from several congressmen, such as Jesse Helms (R-NC), and organizations such as the National Restaurant Association (or, the *other* NRA), the Chapman Amendment eventually lost momentum and was finally soundly defeated in the House, paving the way for the ADA to pass Congress with overwhelming support in mid-summer 1990.

The ADA was signed into law on the East Lawn of the White House on July 26, 1990. President Bush said, "With this law, another shameful wall of prejudice and discrimination comes tumbling

---

13. Young, *Equality of Opportunity*, 90.

down."[14] In a remarkable show of speed and a testimony to how far disability rights had come, the Department of Health, Education, and Welfare (HEW) issued point-by-point regulations for the ADA in early 1991, less than a year after the legislation was enshrined into federal law. This was a poignant reminder of the progress the disability community had made since the early 70s and the Rehabilitation Act, which took over four years to achieve regulatory status.

Living with and Adapting the ADA

The ADA and the fight for civil rights for persons with disabilities remains an ongoing process that is equally full of hope and controversy. To this ongoing process, I briefly turn now. In 2008, the ADA Amendments Act was passed in order to address shortcomings of the bill that have been uncovered through the courts since the Act's original passage in 1990. The necessity of the ADAA, according to Jones, is twofold. First, "Congress never intended that people with very serious impairments (e.g., 'diabetes, epilepsy, heart conditions, cancer, mental illnesses') would be denied ADA protection simply because they continued to function much as do people without such impairments."[15] Second, lawmakers sought to combat the ADA litigation that "had become preoccupied with whether the plaintiff-employee was disabled as opposed to whether the defendant-employer had engaged in unlawful discrimination."[16] Basically, the first concern of the ADAA focused on clarifying that whether or not a person's disability is mitigated, by medical intervention or other factors, should have no bearing under the ADA as to whether that person is considered disabled; rather, the root impairment is all that is considered. This part of the amendment came out of years of litigation in which in some cases the mitigating factors were taken into consideration and

14. Bush, *Remarks of President George Bush,* 26 July 1990.
15. Jones, "Enfeebling the ADA," 668.
16. Jones, "Enfeebling the ADA," 668.

in some cases they were not. Congress simply wanted to close a loophole. On the second impetus of the ADAA, Congress felt that the ADA had transitioned from legislation that had protected the civil rights of persons with disabilities to legislation that tried to determine whether a litigant was disabled in order to justify a discrimination lawsuit. The ADAA focused much more on whether the person with a disability was discriminated against and in some circumstances lowered the threshold of what actually constitutes disability under the law.

The second piece of noteworthy legislation introduced since the ADA is known as the Twenty-First Century Communications and Video Accessibility Act of 2010 (CVAA). The CVAA is meant to ensure that as the pace of technological change increases in the United States, the disabled community is able to have access. The Act puts safeguards in place to require that any newly developed communication technology must have disability accessibility in mind during development. Although there have been questions about whether the CVAA preempts the ADA, and whether brick-and-mortar retailers with web commerce outlets fall under its requirements, the CVAA seems to be a step in the right direction.[17]

There is one more relatively recent development in the legislative life of the Americans with Disabilities Act. At the time of the writing of this book, there is currently in committee within the House of Representatives a possible amendment to the Americans with Disabilities Act introduced by representative Ted Poe, Republican of Texas: House Resolution 620 ADA Education and Reform Act of 2017, which ostensibly would require the Department of Justice to develop programs and strategies for business owners and state and local governments regarding full and equal access for persons with disabilities. On the surface, this sounds like a decent amendment, but as they say, the devil really is in the details. According to portions of the bill's summary on the US government website:

17. Burks, "Improving Access," 363.

The bill prohibits civil actions based on the failure to remove an architectural barrier to access into an existing public accommodation unless: (1) the aggrieved person has provided to the owners or operators a written notice specific enough to identify the barrier, and (2) the owners or operators fail to provide the person with a written description outlining improvements that will be made to improve the barrier or they fail to remove the barrier or make substantial progress after providing such a description. The aggrieved person's notice must specify: (1) the address of the property, (2) the specific ADA sections alleged to have been violated, (3) whether a request for assistance in removing an architectural barrier was made, and (4) whether the barrier was permanent or temporary.

In the opinion of this author, this proposed amendment places much of the burden regarding the ADA on those whom it is intended to protect. You would never ask someone who is actively being discriminated against to point it out in order to trigger anti-discrimination laws. In effect, this is what that HR 620 appears to be doing. We will have to watch carefully to see how this development progresses through the legislative journey.[18] Despite many notable attempts, both within and without the federal government, to ensure the inclusion of people with disabilities, there are still areas in which much work remains. Sadly, one of those areas is communities of faith. One of the strangest facts about the Americans with Disabilities Act is its Ministerial Exception. "Simply put, this means that if an employee is classified as a 'minister,' that employee is not entitled to the protections of the ADA."[19] The original intention of this exception is to prevent the federal

---

18. Author's note: As of April 6, 2018, this law appears to be permanently killed in the US Senate where a coalition of 40 Democratic senators led by Tammy Duckworth (D-IL) said they would not vote for it, therefore making it impossible to bring to the Senate floor. See Jonathan Hilburg, "Proposed Rollback of Americans with Disabilities Act is Permanently Stalled," Architects Newspaper, April 6, 2018, https://archpaper.com/2018/04/rollback-americans-with-disabilities-act-stalled/.

19. Taylor, "Special Rules for the Church," 224.

government from interfering or meddling in church affairs, under the ADA, should a minister be found to be engaging in behavior or lifestyle that would contradict church teachings and yet be covered under ADA, vis a vis HIV/AIDS (see above). Whatever one might think of the original intent of the Ministerial Exception, the way in which it has come to be used is far from it.

An example is the *Perich v. Hosanna-Tabor* case, which found its way all the way to the Supreme Court in 2012. A very brief description of the case is as follows: Cheryl Perich was a "called teacher" at Hosanna-Tabor, a school run by the Missouri Synod Lutheran Church in Michigan. This meant that she taught a curriculum of secular subjects along with leading her class in prayer and facilitating chapel one to two times a year. Called teachers were designated so by the congregation connected to the school. There were both called teachers and non-called teachers in the school at the time. The duties of called teachers versus non-called teachers were exactly the same. However, the Missouri Synod Church designated called teachers as ministers.

Sometime between the end of 2004 and the beginning of 2005, Ms. Perich was diagnosed with narcolepsy. She subsequently informed the administrator at the school that she would need to take a leave of absence to receive treatment. She later informed the administrator that her treatment had gone well and she would be able to return to school in time for the beginning of the next semester. Ms. Perich was informed that a replacement had been found for her position, and the congregation was reviewing its workers' compensation policy to insert a provision that anyone on leave for longer than six months would be asked to resign. Ms. Perich informed school administrators that she would be able to return to school at the end of February 2005, two days after this email. School administrators met with the congregation to inform them that Ms. Perich would not be able to return to school this year or the next. Ms. Perich returned to school on the day that she had indicated only to be told to leave and to be later informed that she would be fired for causing a disturbance when she returned to school.

She filed a lawsuit with the help of the Equal Opportunity Employment Office, but lost because the court ruled that she was a minister, which placed her under the Ministerial Exception of the ADA. Eventually, after several rounds in the higher courts, the case went all the way to the Supreme Court, in which the justices ruled in favor of Hosanna-Tabor, based on the Ministerial Exception. I encourage you to read more in-depth into the facts of this case, as I can only provide the shortest of summaries. The appalling nature of this case becomes even more devastating when one considers that, with a few exceptions, a majority of the major Christian denominations and other religious organizations in the United States filed briefs in support of the Hosanna-Tabor school. A partial list is as follows: the American Jewish Committee, the Union of Orthodox Jewish Congregations of America, the Union for Reform Judaism, the United States Conference of Catholic Bishops, the Episcopal Church, the Evangelical Lutheran Church in America, the United Methodist Church, the United Church of Christ, the Presbyterian Church (U.S.A.), the Evangelical Covenant Church, the Seventh-Day Adventists, the Southern Baptist Convention, the Foursquare Gospel Church, the Salvation Army National Corporation, InterVarsity Christian Fellowship/USA, the Church of Jesus Christ of Latter-day Saints, the Council of Hindu Temples of North America, the International Society for Krishna Consciousness, the Muslim-American Public Affairs Council, the United Sikhs, the Church of the Lukumi Babalu Aye, and Templo Yoruba Omo Orisha.[20] While there were agencies and religious organizations that were supportive of Cheryl Perich, sadly this list was not nearly as long or as powerful.

Conclusion

For years, growing up as a United Methodist, going to youth group and being involved in the church, I never really understood the anger I felt from the disability community toward the church.

20. Taylor, "Special Rules for the Church," 232.

Now, with violent clarity, I understand the feeling of many in the disabled community that much of Christian hospitality appears to be lip service while true access and community often comes down to budget decisions, historical building committees, and church bureaucracy, which will ultimately lead to those within the disability community feeling further isolation.

This case illustrates why my wife and I feel an intentional Christian community that incorporates both the nondisabled and the disabled is so vitally important. Jesus Christ came to be in community and bring salvation to people, not resolve issues. The church cannot truly make disciples for the transformation of the world if it continues to be on the wrong side of history and humanity, and to, at times, reject the people it is trying to reach.

The thing we must come to know, as people of faith, is that disability is not just one issue among many in our lives. In many cases, it is integral to the very way we view our existence. Yes, disability is a struggle. My Cerebral Palsy is a struggle. It's also something I am very, very proud of. I invite the church to live with us and to know us as people. Hopefully, by studying the civil rights struggle of people with disabilities, we will begin to understand the God-given potential and faithfulness that people with disabilities possess and want to share with the world.

3

An Examination of Theology
and Its Impact

THE HISTORY OF CHRISTIAN theology is a history of human beings, primarily men, saying things about God and God's relationship to humankind. Often, when important theological statements
are made, they occur in the context of highly nuanced, complex
arguments or conversations. The further one proceeds from the
origin of the conversation, the less nuance surrounds a statement.
For example, Augustine's highly nuanced argument on the origin
of sin and its consequences eventually becomes something in the
neighborhood of "sex is bad and people are wretches." Or, Martin
Luther King's explosive and revolutionary message of social justice and radical change becomes "I have a dream." Reflecting on
the past, we are often left with a sound bite, the easiest and, often, the most dramatic part of a theological statement, with very
little nuance and context. What this process inevitably leads to is
a modern-day theological framework built on an interpretation of
a theological heritage that is radically different from the original
intentions of the theologians who proposed the ideas.

This dynamic also has particular potency when one examines
the effect that our theological forbearers have on the discussion
surrounding disability theology and its modern day consequences
and context. Before considering what others have said, it feels only

right that I take a moment and inform you, the reader, just what the undergirding principles of disability theology are in my understanding. First, all humans are made in the image of God and are thus very good creations. Disability does not inherently mar the image of God in any person. Second, in the life, death, and resurrection of Jesus Christ, we see God Incarnate in a human form that manifests disability in many ways. In particular, Jesus' resurrected body still manifests the wounds of crucifixion, which is the same body that is taken up into heaven. Thus, disability has a part in the life of Jesus as Savior and the life of the Triune God. Third, Paul identifies the Christian community as the Body of Christ in many of his letters. All Christians participate in the Body of Christ and have their roles to play in the work of God's kingdom (kin-dom) on earth as it is in heaven. If the resurrected body of Christ manifests disability, there's no reason the kin-dom of God should not do the same.

Through an examination of St. Augustine, Friedrich Schleiermacher, and Karl Barth, I hope to demonstrate how historical theological ideas and concepts are still shaping and dominating the way many Christians think about (or don't think about) what we say about the human body, the human intellect, and the human soul. These conversations have often had and continue to have a profoundly damaging impact for those living with a wide range of what we would historically call disabling conditions. As we move forward into engaging these three theologians in particular, I would ask you to keep in mind that my goal is not necessarily to correct or condemn the theology that we will evaluate and consider. However, one would do well to keep in mind the three foundational principles that I have just articulated and place them in dialogue with the theologians that we will meet in the forthcoming pages. Before beginning, I would like to note that I am intending to cite instances that are specifically pertinent and relevant to the discussion of disability and, when I note that something is problematic or troubling, it is not intended to undermine the person's entire corpus but simply to draw attention to discussions that are germane to disability.

Augustine of Hippo

The impact of Augustine of Hippo's theology on the development of Western Christian theology cannot be overstated. Whether one swims with the tide of Augustine's thought or against it, Augustine is an essential theological figure in Western Christianity and must be addressed when considering Christian theology in general and the body in particular.

In *Disability in the Christian Tradition*, writer and editor Brian Brock acknowledges two dominant thought systems regarding the human physical condition in Augustine's works. First, "a minor but highly suggestive strand of [Augustine's] thought emphasizes the ways in which our perception of other human beings must be illuminated or sanctified if we are to know them rightly and resist the temptation to approach people as little more than their apparent deficits of mind or body."[1] Second, a more dominant form of Augustine's theological reflection concerns "the perfection of the human body and mind."[2]

In *City of God* XIX.4, these two streams of thought intermingle as Augustine argues against the Stoic philosophers, who were Augustine's contemporaries and intellectual rivals, who say that the Ultimate Good is found in this earthly life and whatever befalls humans in this life is Good. Augustine brilliantly points out a flaw in this position when he asks, "But what if some disorder causes the limbs to tremble? What if a man's spine is so curved as to bring his hands to the ground, so that he becomes a kind of quadruped? Will this not subvert all the body's beauty and grace, whether it be at rest or in motion?"[3] While this passage will strike modern readers as odd, cold, or maybe even cruel, it actually contains an expertly crafted argument against the Stoic philosophers. He points out that the philosophers hold an untenable position when they uphold that the ultimate good is found in this earthly life while simultaneously arguing that if some illness or overwhelming

1. Bock, "Augustine's Hierarchies," 65.
2. Bock, "Augustine's Hierarchies," 65–66.
3. Augustine of Hippo, "*The City of God*, XIX.4," 90.

catastrophe occurs, it is not beyond reason for an individual to take one's life with serene dignity and stoic fortitude.

By arguing against this interpretation, Augustine moves happiness beyond one's earthly circumstances and physical situation. The novelty of this way of thinking cannot be overstated. However, as much as he would say that happiness is outside of one's present condition and all people are equal in this way, he still refers to disability or malady as a tragic and lamentable circumstance. So, what an individual is left with is this basic argument: This present life is equally lamentable for everyone. Whether one is disabled or nondisabled, there is an equal share of hope in awaiting God's Kingdom.

Augustine's theological approach has been coopted and wildly overextended by many modern day Evangelicals, who declare that the greater share of happiness is located in a heavenly hereafter, and that heavenly reality should be considered the ultimate reality. It is very easy for a physically normative cultural framework to talk about being less concerned with earthly reality, because they do not have to deal with the day-to-day embodied impact of disability. We have moved forward with a theology that, while leveling the playing field philosophically, does nothing to redeem the language of disability nor the theological vantage point of those living with the disabled experience.

Augustine did try to overturn the prevailing notions about disability: that those who were born with disabilities were under some divine retribution or were suffering an existence totally devoid of the ability to connect with any sort of spirituality whatsoever. For example, in *A Treatise on the Merits and Forgiveness of Sins, and on the Baptism of Infants,* Augustine discusses a man of diminished mental capacity whom he describes as a fool and a Christian. Here, he uses the Greek word for moron (*moros*) in its proper context to describe someone of diminished mental faculty. Augustine describes the man as "patient to the degree of strange folly"[4] except when it comes to anyone who would blaspheme the

---

4. Augustine of Hippo, "A Treatise on the Merits and Forgiveness of Sins," 79.

name of God. It's important to take note that Augustine gives the individual credit for being aware of the divine in ways that were perhaps not as common in the prevailing thought and theology of his day. However, he still makes the man's apparent cognitive deficits a hindrance or an obstacle to be overcome, instead of a normative part of God's diverse creation.

While it must be said that Augustine was ahead of his time in encouraging people to evaluate the whole of human experience as useful and important to God, one does not have to look very far to discover potentially troubling implications for disability in Augustine's larger corpus. One only has to examine the way he usually approaches the relationship between man's body and mind or soul in general. When, in *Confessions*, Augustine traces his spiritual journey of ascension to relationship with God, he begins in a place of sensual habits, progresses to the level of the intellect or mutable mind, and finally arrives at a place of the soul or a more celestial, eternal realm.

Beneath Augustine's high-flown rhetoric and transcendent descriptions, one may discern his assertion that humans can only interpret the things of the soul through their bodies and physical senses. By setting things forth in this way, Augustine immediately creates a hierarchical structure of feeling concerning human experience and life within God. Although this argument is a masterpiece of rhetoric and a highly complex and subtle description of the burgeoning of Augustine's spiritual life, here we have a prime example of the way in which a highly nuanced thought can get out of hand if succeeding generations of interpreters do not maintain the subtlety and nuance. The argument Augustine makes about his dawning knowledge of God, beginning in his central feelings and progressing to his mind and soul, was very important to Augustine because he understood the conversion experience as someone with a background in the fourth-century Greco-Roman philosophical thought would. Augustine was interpreting a deeply important experience through the filter he most readily understood. When the specificity and intimacy of Augustine's situation is forgotten and we make the hierarchy of body, mind, and soul into a systematic philosophical move, rather than a filter for an individual experience, this is where the church finds itself in trouble generations down the road.

Augustine continues to employ hierarchy as a way of understanding human existence in *City of God* when he states that "those which have life are placed above those which do not . . . the sentient are placed above those which do not have sensation . . . Among the sentient, the intelligent are placed above those which do not have intelligence."[5]

I could probably spend hours going through the list of grievous consequences that derive from theologies based around statements like this. Of course, one cannot look past the connection that was formed between the person's ability to reason and the perception of their quality of life. Many of the atrocities of the Holocaust were based on this very thing. Yet, while that is a worthwhile area of research and writing, I would prefer to look at the ramifications of Augustine's work as it exists today, or, at least, as it exists from where I sit as an individual with a disability.

If an individual were so inclined, one could ask the question, "What is meant by 'sensation' or 'sentience'?" Does an individual's quality of life and ability to connect to God become radically impaired when he or she loses feeling in his or her leg due to Diabetes or experiences significant visual impairment like Daniel, a member of The Julian Way we will meet in the final section of this book? Should the theological contribution of those with intellectual disabilities be discounted due to their lack of reason or reason as we know it?

I do not want to lay all blame for the church's lack of engagement with disability firmly at the feet of Augustine. That is not only irresponsible; it is dangerously inaccurate. As we will see later, there is plenty of responsibility to go around.

To see the legacy of Augustine's devaluation of the body and therefore the ability of the body, I would simply call the church's attention to the level of priority that the church gives to ministry with those people with disabilities. When I say this, I do not mean

5. Augustine of Hippo, "*The City of God*, XI.16 (470)," 87.

simply respite care situations or a Sunday school class for those with mental and physical challenges, I mean ministries driven and created by and through those with unique physical and developmental embodiments. I would contend that, although we never phrase it like this, because of a current love for ministries, programs, and even perhaps people who are "bigger, faster, stronger, and more exciting," the church is still operating well within Augustine's hierarchical structure.

There have been others who have had the opportunity along the way to correct the course but who, for a number of reasons, did not. We now continue the discussion with two such individuals.

Friedrich Schleiermacher

Moving forward several centuries, we encounter an individual, Friedrich Schleiermacher, who in his own way did as much to shape the theological climate of the early twentieth century as did anyone else. In fact, some would say that the theologian we will encounter next, Karl Barth, spent his career in a decades-long counterargument with Friedrich Schleiermacher. In a life spanning a relatively brief sixty-five years, Schleiermacher's works mark the beginning of the era of Protestant Liberal Theology.[6] Through his efforts to articulate Christianity to his friends and social peers in the elite of German society, Schleiermacher almost single-handedly developed new conceptions of faith, the Incarnation, and Christology. As with most of the theologians we will explore, Schleiermacher rarely, if ever, touches directly on the topic of disability, although we do see slightly more direct engagement with it in his theological corpus. Even with this direct engagement, one is still left largely to draw on general statements of theology to construct what we now call a theology of disability.

Before delving into the particulars of Schleiermacher's theology, it is helpful to understand Schleiermacher's particular characterization of "religious feeling." Schleiermacher does

6. Forstman, Foreword to *On Religion*, viii.

not understand religious feeling as an emotion or mood with a religious focus. Rather, religious feeling is a unique "eternal and universal state of consciousness" which can only be generated by God.[7] Therefore, a primary source of theology for Schleiermacher is religious feeling: the interior interaction of the self and God unmediated by any exterior sources. Thus, Schleiermacher conceives of a truly religious life as moving from a faith built on exterior ritual and practice to a faith filled with a greater knowledge of the interior response and transformational power of Christ.

This interplay between the interior and exterior is reflected in Schleiermacher's sermon of 1810 on the conversion of St. Paul. In addition to the externally miraculous aspect of Paul's conversion, Schleiermacher claims that the most important aspect of Paul's conversion event is what Christ was doing to Paul through "the inner origin of [Paul's] conviction."[8] In an essay on the 1810 sermon, Christopher Anderson reinforces Schleiermacher's focus on the interior experience of Paul when he makes the point that Schleiermacher interprets Paul's blindness as a "symbol of the complete falling away of the exterior in the work of salvation."[9]

This offers both helpful and harmful possibilities for those with disabilities. To illustrate this, we will once again consider a member of The Julian Way, twelve-year-old Jimmy, who deals with Cerebral Palsy. On the one hand Schleiermacher's emphasis on the interior nature of faith allows an opportunity for Jimmy and other individuals with disabilities to freely approach Christ and Christ's work without reference to their physical state, which is so much a part of other dominant theological strands. While the case can be made that many of the Desert Fathers and Mothers similarly focused on the interior life of religious experience, Schleiermacher uniquely assumes religious feeling as the starting point for theology and faithful Christian life. In *On Religion*, Schleiermacher defines religion as the seeking of "the immediate consciousness of the universal existence of all finite things, in and through the

7. Dumbreck, *Schleiermacher and Religious Feeling*, xi.
8. Anderson, "Felix Mendelssohn und Friedrich Schleiermacher," 159–62.
9. Anderson, "Felix Mendelssohn und Friedrich Schleiermacher," 159–62.

Infinite, and of all temporal things in and through the Eternal." He goes on to say that religion is found "in all that lives and moves, in all growth and change, in all doing and suffering."[10] Essentially, God is Infinite, and, if we place ourselves in contemplation of the Infinite, we, who are finite, will eventually come to a better un-derstanding of God and also ourselves in relation to God. This is potentially freeing for persons with disabilities because it liberates us from the consideration of certain embodiments as hindrances to faithful religious life.

As I have stated above, I think the internalizing of religious experience can be helpful to those with disabilities because of its offering disabled persons opportunities to express their religious faith in ways that are not so immediately tied to external, physical situations or circumstances. I do want to caution against separat-ing religious experience too far from physicality, because to do this as a person with a disability one runs the risk of falling into a type of Gnosticism, a heresy that seeks to divorce spirituality from the body.

When interacting with Schleiermacher, it is important to remember that he lived in a time of great faith in human prog-ress, before the concept and reality of suffering were brought to a global scale with the mechanized war and industrialization of the early twentieth century. To put it succinctly, Schleiermacher simply had no concept for articulating the violence and brutality that humans would have the capability to inflict upon one another. Schleiermacher's belief in progress is evident when you consider how much weight he puts on finite human beings contemplating God. Schleiermacher allows for substantial human involvement in his framework of faith where individuals are not just passive recipients, but active parts of the equation. We see a similar move when Schleiermacher reiterates that individuals seek God "in all that lives and moves, in all growth and change, in all doing and suffering."[11] Here again, we see that aspects of God run through all of life, and human beings can glimpse God in all of life's progress.

10. Schleiermacher, *On Religion*, 36.

11. Schleiermacher, *On Religion*, 36.

One gets the sense that when Schleiermacher is talking of "growth and change," and even of "doing and suffering," he is referring to a movement of ultimately positive progress. Yet, how do we understand God if our life experiences do not seem to show any positive progress? Although it is ideal to imagine that every moment in the life of a person with disabilities is an opportunity to see something of the divine, this emphasis on positive progress and human ability creates a theology that is not helpful when applied to the nagging aches, pains, and non-progress that can often play a significant part in the life of someone with a disability. Such considerations of a narrative towards eternal progress are made all the more intriguing when one considers that, in fact, Schleiermacher did deal with significant visual impairment, a condition that we would label as disabling today.

Up to this point, we have discussed the emphasis on interior religious understanding in Schleiermacher's work, and the simultaneously helpful and harmful possibilities this emphasis creates for disability theology. Yet, it would only be theologically responsible to consider for a moment the role of those with cognitive, developmental, and emotional difficulties in a system of a faith that is overwhelmingly reliant on contemplation and the interior senses. On a positive note, there is room to consider that those persons with an interior experience that is considered outside the "norm" can still find a religious experience that is of equal value to any other simply because it is *their* own interior experience. On the other hand, until local churches and faith leaders begin to value alternative experiences *and* expressions of religious feeling within faith bodies, Schleiermacher's framework becomes a means to discriminate against cognitive, developmental, and emotional impairments.

Further positive contributions Schleiermacher makes to disability theology are found in his language for sin and the desire for God. Kevin W. Hector, in his article "Actualism and Incarnation: The High Christology of Friedrich Schleiermacher," reminds us that Schleiermacher thought that humans were essentially made up of "the God-consciousness and the sensuous self-consciousness, and in each of us, as a result of our participation in the sinful corporate life, the God-consciousness is subordinated to the sensuous self-consciousness."[12]

For Schleiermacher, "God's existence can only be apprehended as pure activity," and since human beings are not God, every individual's "existence is merely an intermingling of activity and passivity."[13] In the intermingling of activity and passivity in each individual, the "God-consciousness" is the part of us that longs for and connects with the pure activity of God. Thus, the only way that humans can have any real experience of the divine within them is through a human with a constant and consistent God-consciousness, namely Jesus Christ.[14] Further, the pure activity of God is love, which Schleiermacher defines as "the impulse to unite self with neighbor and to will to be in neighbor," or in the case of God's ultimate love, "the union of the Divine Essence with human nature."[15]

In the Incarnation, Christ's God-consciousness "functions as the organ by which God's pure act is apprehended and turned into Christ's own activity."[16] Through the Incarnation, the experience of God's pure activity of love is made accessible to *all* persons. If one chose to view this interpretation as a theological operating system, then the consequences for the disabled community would be profound. Imagine for a moment if the most dramatic expression of God's pure life in somebody is love. It would stand to reason that one would not need to be physically healed to be a dramatic picture of the power of Christ. Rather, one needs only to know they are loved by God, and be able to articulate that love to others in order to be a miracle in this world. Such knowledge lies beyond simple cognitive understanding or recognition and has much more to do with the heart. Here again, when I am referring to the ability to articulate that love, I am not speaking exclusively to the

12. Hector, "Actualism and Incarnation," 311.

13. Schleiermacher, *Christian Faith*, 387.

14. Hector, "Actualism and Incarnation," 311–12.

15. Schleiermacher, *Christian Faith*, 726–27.

16. Hector, "Actualism and Incarnation," 311.

intellectual ability to articulate. More, that one is able to articulate the love God through the life they lead and the presence they have in the lives of those they know.

As was pointed out at the beginning of this discussion, the work of Friedrich Schleiermacher is largely considered the starting point of modern Liberal Protestantism "especially in relation to his emphasis upon human 'feeling' . . . and the need to relate Christian faith to the human situation."[17] However, major stumbling blocks in Schleiermacher's theology arise from his heavy dependence on the interior experience of the human that often seems to downplay the physical and to demystify the miraculous. These stumbling blocks are certainly present when trying to facilitate a conversation between Schleiermacher and disability theology, which affirms both that there is nothing about disability that inherently separates one from relationship or communion with God and that the physical embodiment of disability serves as a signpost for God's creativity in the world. I have spent many of the preceding paragraphs discussing positive steps for the disabled where Schleiermacher is concerned. However, Schleiermacher's language is so nuanced and convoluted that one is left with few resources for how to translate the concepts of Schleiermacher into meaningful, day-to-day Christian interactions. Where there is potential for freedom in affirming the relationship between God and all individuals, no matter their physical, cognitive, or emotional circumstances, Schleiermacher does not provide the means for interpreting the potentially life-giving consequences of this theological stance within the corporate life of the church. It is a laudable desire to affirm that a person's interior experience of faith allows them to be fully included in God's kingdom and plan. However, until we find a way to move beyond inclusion in God to participation in God, the benefit of Schleiermacher's work on interior experience and God's pure activity of love will result in nothing more than paper cathedrals that will crumble around persons with disabilities with the first wind and rain of physical life experience. Sadly, this is

17. McGrath, *Christian Theology*, 101.

what many modern-day congregations have done with the legacy of Schleiermacher.

Karl Barth

There is perhaps no more influential Protestant in the twentieth century than Karl Barth. He began his theological career in the happy, idyllic days of the late nineteenth and early twentieth centuries, where the march of human progress seemed to come together perfectly with the move towards theological optimism. As with many other great thinkers of his era, this happy illusion was completely obliterated with the advent of World War I. Some might say that Barth spent the remainder of his life helping the world awaken from its dreams and come to a realistic sense of Christ's work in the world and of the hope offered to humankind through that work. As with Schleiermacher before him, building a disability theology that correlates directly with Barth's work is fiendishly difficult to accomplish, given the fact that Barth scarcely addressed disability directly in any substantive way within his corpus, and, certainly, not at all within his crowning achievement, *Church Dogmatics*. This leaves theologians and authors, such as myself and those with considerably more talent, to build a disability theology around what Barth says about sickness, the human experience, and the centrality of Christ.

Perhaps one of the more progressive statements Barth makes about disability comes in a fairly well-known conversation between him and fellow theologian Heinrich Vogel. Author David Wood recounts this dialogue within *Disability in the Christian Tradition*. He admits that the conversation comes in several versions, some of which conflict, but I believe that the anecdote is still very informative. Vogel, whose daughter was both profoundly physically and cognitively impaired, spoke from his expectation and desire as a father in saying, "She will walk!" The account given in Wood's essay contains the following response from Barth:

No, that makes it sound as if God has made a mistake in
your daughter's case, one which he is obliged to put right.
Is it not a much more beautiful and powerful hope . . .
that something becomes apparent there that at present
we cannot understand at all—namely that this life was
not futile, because it is not in vain that God has said to it:
"I have loved: you!"?[18]

Within this quotation is much fertile soil, out of which might grow
a theology that moves past the use of disability as a way to prove
a person's holiness, particular giftedness, or as a source of divine
curse or retribution. In fact, one might say that Barth may be leav-
ing the door open for a theology that allows those things seen in
this life as impairments to remain fully intact in God's Kingdom,
but this time, in their fully revealed and glorified state.

Perhaps I can use myself as an example to further clarify this
point. While it is not a matter for argument that my Cerebral Palsy
can and often does pose physical and social challenges in daily life,
often requiring creative solutions, it is also beyond doubt (at least
to me) that my Cerebral Palsy has done much to inform my character as an individual and has become a proud part of who I continue
to grow to be, both as a man and in the context of my relationship
with Jesus Christ. I give Barth credit for creating an environment,
at least in some respects, for this theology to be developed.

Although there is much to be admired and gleaned from
this conversation (or at least the version we have before us), there
are still portions of Barth's theology, particularly around sickness,
health, and the human will that can lead to troubling conclusions.

It is in exploring this aspect that we will spend the remainder
of our time with Karl Barth. In the third volume of *Church Dogmatics*, Barth seems to say that man and man's soul can be examined
in two coexistent parts: the "rational soul of his . . . animal body"
and the "ruling soul of his serving body."[19] I take "animal body"
to mean, in Barth's language, the physical human experience, and
"ruling soul of his serving body" to be more closely connected

18. Wood, "*This* Ability," 392.
19. Barth, "*Church Dogmatics* III/4, 357–9," 415.

to the spiritual existence. While I am ready to admit this reading might be slightly over-simplistic, I do believe it is good to be getting on with.

Later in this same section, Barth makes the statement that, "Health and sickness in the two do not constitute two divided realms, but are always a single whole . . . he lives the healthy or sick life of his body together with that of his soul, and again in both cases, and in their mutual relationship, it is a matter of his life's history, his own history, and therefore himself."[20] Let me say with some degree of clarity and forcefulness that I sincerely believe that if Karl Barth were able to respond within this conversation directly, that he would say that physical disability or ailment do not have anything to do with the human capacity to love and be in relationship with God. This is, at least, my sincere hope. What one is presented with in *Church Dogmatics*, however, seems to be a dramatic conflation of body and soul that would run the risk of concluding that someone's physical and spiritual health are so nearly tied together that they have an almost correlative relationship. As was stated moments ago, I would hope with nuance and shading to be able to discover that this was not fully what Barth meant, but given that we are only left with words on the page, one has to use what is at hand.

The conversation and situation gets murkier still if one endeavors to discover the connection Barth seems to make between human will, in both the physical and spiritual realm, and the relationship between health and sickness. Looking again at Volume III of *Church Dogmatics*, Barth writes:

> If health is the strength for human existence, even those who are seriously ill can will to be healthy without any optimism or illusions regarding their condition. They, too, are commanded, and it is not too much to ask, that so long as they are alive they should will this, i.e., exercise the power which remains to them, in spite of every obstacle.[21]

20. Barth, "*Church Dogmatics* III/4, 357–9," 415–16.
21. Barth, "*Church Dogmatics* III/4, 357–9," 415.

I must confess that there is in my mind more potential trouble in this statement than in almost anything else that I have come across while writing this work so far. Barth seems to say that those who are ill should and can will to be healthy, and, if they do so, they will attain to more health than they currently possess or exhibit. Again, I am deeply concerned, not so much with what Barth says directly, but rather where it leads. If a person remains in sickness and/or physical disability, should we will to be better? What are we left with? One of those people we will meet in the closing portion of this work, a man named Steve Clark, deals with Parkinson's Disease, a condition that can be at the best slowed through medical intervention. I do not think that Barth would ask Mr. Clark to will to be better. Those who would recklessly follow in Barth's footsteps, however, are the ones who would worry me.

Perhaps this argument or statement implies so much danger for me because I have seen its consequences. I have experienced people in church leadership, in varying contexts, speak to the disabled as though their condition were a deficit or a lack, and they should desire healing or wholeness because they believe that health is a matter of will. Frankly, it distresses me to think that someone so renowned would make statements, even if only in appearance, that seem to say that sickness, illness, and ailment are so closely correlated to the human will.

This statement is doubly and triply shocking when one considers the above account of the conversation with Heinrich Vogel. That someone can show such profound pastoral instincts combined with wise theological acumen in this one situation, and then make statements such as the ones we have just examined and leave them for posterity to play with as though they are theological nitroglycerin is at the very least deeply troubling. This is perhaps most perplexing when one considers that this is the man that was primarily responsible for the foundational document of the confessing church in Germany, The Barmen Declaration, the 1934 document that detailed in no small part the Christian response to Nazi Germany and the atrocities against Jews and those with disabilities. One has to wonder how the two statements can come from one pen, especially when considering how much of Nazi ideology was based on the concept that physical deformity meant spiritual and rational corruption.

The value that these three giants of the church have had when it comes to developing the conversation around how we live out our faith as people of God cannot be underestimated. However, one must wrestle with the very real consequences that have come from investing three individuals, not to mention others, with such foundational weight and power to shape theology down through the centuries, when the things they said and statements they made regarding individuals with disabilities have left us with so many unanswered and troubling questions in our current theological context.

Moving forward from this point, we will begin to examine theologians and people of the Church who have much more direct bearing on intentional Christian community and disability theology. We will be engaging in conversation with people both old and relatively new. To begin this part of our journey, we will explore the contributions of three men who in very different ways offer their perspectives on disability and disability theology. These men are Jean Vanier, Henri Nouwen, and Stanley Hauerwas.

4

Developments and Movement within Disability Theology

VANIER, HAUERWAS, AND NOUWEN are in many ways inextricably linked to one another. Because of their relationship, the Christian church has in many ways been introduced to individuals with disabilities in ways not previously done.

Jean Vanier

Without a doubt, the man most responsible for introducing individuals with disabilities to the Christian church is Jean Vanier. This unassuming and deeply compassionate Catholic man, who at one time was considering a calling to the priesthood while enjoying a successful and rapidly advancing career in the Royal Canadian Navy, gave all of that up to live among individuals with severe intellectual and developmental disabilities in a small French village. When the L'Arche communities began in 1964, they weren't communities at all. It was just Jean Vanier, a small house, and three men with profound disabilities. In her book *The Miracle, The Message, The Story: Jean Vanier and l'Arche*, Kathryn Spink says that the decision to live with these three "broken, rejected people" was an irreversible decision, and the community that arose from this decision was a place where the disabled and nondisabled lived together "not as 'educators' and people with disabilities, but as sharers in a life of communion." Through this communion, L'Arche shows the world the divide between "the strong and the weak, the powerful and the vulnerable, the clever and the disabled, between those with a voice in human affairs and those with none."[1]

From this small stone house in France has sprung an international network of communities in dozens of countries and contexts throughout the world. Jean Vanier and the L'Arche communities have undoubtedly been places of grace, faith, and belonging for individuals dealing with mental and developmental disabilities from around the globe. Of all the sections in this book so far, the section examining the work and contribution of Jean Vanier has been most difficult for me to write simply because I have such great respect for the work of the L'Arche communities. This can make looking at Vanier and L'Arche with a critical eye somewhat challenging. I will do my best to do this with honesty and sensitivity, and with full understanding of how much L'Arche means to those with disabilities and to the church in general.

The fundamental guiding spiritual principle of L'Arche is based on Jesus's teaching in the Beatitudes, particularly around the poor in spirit. The ethos of L'Arche is that, in a concrete sense, the disabled are usually poor, so that in order to live with them in community and relationship, one must share in their poverty.[2] Vanier believes that we are able to see Jesus and the gospel message clearly in those with developmental disabilities because of their inherent poverty of spirit and because of their actual poverty.

Vanier goes on to say that one of the things that the core residents of L'Arche do is allow their assistants who come to serve them to break out of the mentality of seeing their service as solely a matter of doing something for the residents. He says the core residents, which is the term L'Arche uses for their long-term residents with disabilities, allow their assistants to let go of the power inherent in being the helper and come to understand that they, the

1. Spink, *The Miracle, The Message, The Story,* Kindle edition, location 35.
2. Reinders, "Being with the Disabled," 473.

helpers, have something to receive from the core members: the ability to recognize their own weaknesses and shortcomings and find Jesus within relationship with one another. Through his years of work, Vanier has come to believe strongly that the residents of L'Arche can, in a very real sense, be Jesus for their assistants. A quote from his book, *Community and Growth*, sums this up:

> Jesus calls his disciples not only to serve the poor but to discover in them his real presence, a meeting with the Father. Jesus tells us that he is hidden in the face of the poor, that he is in fact the poor. And so with the power of the Spirit, the smallest gesture of love towards the least significant person is a gesture of love towards him.[3]

Vanier contends that those with developmental disabilities are some of the greatest teachers that the church has available because of their ability to instruct others in how to remain in the present moment. He says they are not living in the past or for a future, but are solely dependent on what happens in this moment. Through this quality, those with disabilities teach us to let go of our longing for something else and to see Jesus in the here and the now.

A consistent theme within Vanier's work and life is how those with profound disabilities not only show us Jesus in a very solid and incarnate way, but through their suffering and physical experience, reveal to us a pathway to touch and know our own vulnerability and doubt. In his book *Befriending the Stranger*, Vanier tells the story of Lucien, a man with profound disabilities who, after losing his mother, the only person who ever really knew his wants, needs, and desires, comes to live in the community at La Forestière. When describing the effects that Lucien's screams had on him and the rest of the staff, Vanier says,

> The pitch of Lucien's scream was piercing and seemed to penetrate the very core of my being, awakening my inner anguish. I could sense anger, violence, and even hatred rising up within me. I would have been capable

---

3. Reinders, "Being with the Disabled," 486.

of hurting him to keep him quiet. It was as if a part of my being that I had learned to control was exploding. It was not only Lucien's anguish that was difficult for me to accept but the revelation of what was inside my own heart—my capacity to hurt others—I who had been called to share my life with the weak, had a power of hatred for a weak person![4]

Just as before, Vanier seems to heavily depend on the presence of those with disabilities to teach and inform those who have contact with him. In this quote, he seems to imply that the raw emotion and woundedness of Lucien allowed him to access frustration, anguish, and violence that in other circumstances would have remained hidden from him through self-control and reasoned response. Essentially, God broke down Vanier's walls through one who had no walls he could construct around himself.

Vanier continues talking about walls in his other work, *Living Gently in a Violent World: The Prophetic Witness of Weakness*. He says it is a revelation in the life of a person with a disability when you tell them they have value, that there is something disabled people can say to our society. "In some mysterious way, they are calling to me, to us all, to change."[5] Vanier talks about the walls that go up in our society between those with money and without money and those with power and without. People with disabilities help us find a way to express that the "other" is important, that people are precious and unique. This is the change that Christ wants to lead us to, and the real way to break down walls in our world.

The life of Jean Vanier and his work are invaluable. He was building community with individuals with disabilities long before this issue emerged in any real way on the global consciousness. To try to get a full picture of Vanier's life and work in a few pages is literally an impossibility. This is a man of great nuance, insight, and vision. However, though a genuine motive of love and compassion

---

4. Vanier, *Befriending the Stranger*, Kindle edition, location 1545.
5. Vanier, "The Vision of Jesus," Kindle edition, location 485.

exists, Vanier's work can lead to some troubling outcomes if not considered with a great deal of nuance.

First of all, Jean Vanier was so revolutionary and cutting-edge for his time that all of those who came after him, including Nouwen and Hauerwas, who we will explore later, seem to be reacting to him and through him rather than engaging his work critically to look for next steps and progress. Furthermore, I am somewhat troubled that so much of Vanier's framework has to do with the disabled being closely identified with the poor. For clarification's sake, let me say as a United Methodist pastor and someone who is deeply committed to monastic spirituality, I firmly believe in Jesus' preferential option for the poor and vulnerable. Yet I worry about Vanier's constant characterization of the disabled as poor and vulnerable, not allowing for any other vision or description of God's reality to come forth.

In Kathryn Spink's wonderful biography of Vanier and the story of L'Arche, *The Miracle, The Message, The Story*, Vanier tells us that he has come to understand, particularly in the last few years, that helping the disabled realize as much autonomy and freedom as possible is an extremely important part of the ongoing vision of L'Arche. The difficulty with the overwhelming volume of Vanier's writing referring to the disabled as "poor and vulnerable" is that theologians and authors who have followed in his footsteps have latched on to that part of Vanier's vision to almost total exclusion of any other aspects. I am fully willing to admit that the primary bulk of Vanier's work is with those with mental and developmental disabilities, and this needs to be kept in mind. I don't think Vanier would use so many allusions to vulnerability, suffering, and poverty if he were speaking within a primarily physically disabled context. Although those who have a disability that, like my Cerebral Palsy, is primarily physical certainly face neurological, learning, and developmental challenges, not all who have disabilities would necessarily identify with Vanier's vision. I am concerned that his compelling work might unintentionally trap a wonderfully diverse and rich group of people within one well-intentioned, if limited, version of reality.

Closely related to the problem of only speaking about disability in the context of poverty and vulnerability is that Vanier may be taken to imply, in much of his writings, that the disabled can only teach others through their vulnerability. This leads to a couple of major problems. First and foremost, it can lead to the romanticizing of what for disabled individuals is an often harsh reality. Although in much of Vanier's writings he explicitly warns against this, he cannot control what others do in subsequent writings when the disabled are dramatically envisioned as teaching tools.

Finally, I am concerned that when this viewpoint is given full expression, we begin to view people with mental disabilities through a lens of, "What can they teach me about myself?" I find this situation particularly hard to deal with, because I think Vanier genuinely does strive to help the disabled develop a greater sense of identity within God's kingdom. But, so many of the stories of L'Arche and the encounters we will discover when looking at Nouwen and Hauerwas in particular, have to do with the ways in which the disabled help us to discover things about our own vulnerability and nature. When this happens, you aren't so much helping the disabled discover a sense of intrinsic value as you are making the disabled sense of value dependent on someone else's reality, thereby severely crippling, if not undoing, much of the work Vanier has done.

Henri Nouwen

We will continue our journey in L'Arche with a new companion by tracing the footsteps of Henri Nouwen. Nouwen owes all of his experience in disability theology to his relationship with Jean Vanier and the L'Arche communities in both France and Toronto, Canada. The most prolific period of writing in Henri Nouwen's life is in some way directly tied to L'Arche. Nouwen wrote *Return of the Prodigal Son*, *In the Name of Jesus*, *Adam: God's Beloved*, and *The Road to Daybreak* directly because of his time in L'Arche. For our purposes within this book, we will examine *Adam: God's Beloved* and *The Road to Daybreak* because they deal with the topic of disability explicitly. It is not my intention to address these books in any order of preference or publication. Therefore, I will draw from them each several times.

The Road to Daybreak is the journal of Henri Nouwen during his time in the community of Trosly in France. He had come to Trosly just after being made Professor at Harvard Divinity School in order to find peace and healing after a relationship with a friend had become destructive. *Adam: God's Beloved* is the story of Nouwen's time as an assistant in the New House at L'Arche Daybreak, Toronto, Canada, in 1986–87. In this book, Nouwen tells the story of how Adam, a man with severe epilepsy, transformed his life and became a gateway to deeper relationship and understanding of Jesus Christ.

What strikes me when one looks at Henri Nouwen in the context of L'Arche is his vulnerability. Nouwen came to Trosly in France essentially a man in flight, running from the suffocating nature of an academic environment where God was reduced to a series of intellectual propositions and imperatives. He was also fleeing a relationship that had produced fruit in the past but had become toxic and life-taking instead of life-giving. Nouwen was a man in search of the spiritual peace and source of life that he knew was found in Jesus Christ, but he had slowly lost touch with over the years. Essentially, Nouwen is someone who was broken and deeply vulnerable who came to a place where the most vulnerable and "broken" people were, in order to put himself back together. I am not critical of the fact that Nouwen did this; in fact I think as we read along and explore both of these books we will see that in many ways this was a good move for Henri Nouwen. What I am saying is that I think as we look at primarily *Adam: God's Beloved*, we will see a man primed to see Jesus under every rock and who was understandably yearning for a deep connection with Christ, as he should have been. However, the consequences of this lead to some reckless use of the disabled in the place of Christ.

Nouwen continues, much in the way of Vanier, to identify the disabled with the poor. In his diary, which later became *The Road to Daybreak*, he points out, I believe accurately, that the way of Jesus is the way of the poor, and then says, "Handicapped people are not only poor; they also reveal to us our own poverty. Their primal call is an anguished cry: 'Do you love me?' and 'Why have you forsaken me?'"[6] Here again, I am not trying to imply that many people who deal with physical challenges and intellectual difficulties do not in fact suffer a great deal of anguish and deal with an exquisitely poignant and personal form of pain. However, I think what is dangerous about the leaps Nouwen is making, particularly here, is two-fold.

First, Nouwen assumes that because of the lack of verbal and/or intellectual agency that one can assume a cry of anguish and/or pain is a given. This is a fair and, in some senses, completely valid statement for someone to make in Nouwen's context and in his situation and writing within the pages of his personal journal. The trouble begins when that personal, private journal written by a man dealing with a very personal situation of anguish becomes a published work of a spiritual giant. When this happens, the intimate words of reflection take on an element of canon for all times, all places, and in all situations, and then we are dealing with another instance of the lack of nuance that has haunted so many throughout the history of disability and the church.

Second, he defines the handicapped connection to Jesus and the poor primarily through the lack of something. Again, realizing that whatever I say here requires me to deal in general terms, I feel like this point needs some further clarification. Most often, when we teach about Jesus's beatitude referring to the poor in spirit, we talk of humility. We take for granted that this teaching is meant for a largely nondisabled audience, wherein the coming to poverty or the process of being poor in spirit is assumed to be a much more active decision.

However, in this case, when disability is involved, we have no problem defining poverty from a lack of something because we are assuming that the disabled are denied power that they never had in the first place. What this does is create a glass ceiling of sorts for

6. Nouwen, *Road to Daybreak*, 149.

disabled people, in that we simultaneously ascribe to them Christ-like qualities while in the same breath stripping them of any real active part in the process of moving towards deeper faith. Speaking as a disabled individual, it comes across like this: *My only role in the body of Christ is to draw you closer to God because of what I inherently lack.* This distinction is subtle and may be in some ways hair-splitting; but I believe it is very important because it limits the ways in which the disabled can experience relationship with God and the ways in which the disabled can be of use to the rest of the body of Christ.

Moving now to look closer at Nouwen's writing in *Adam: God's Beloved*, we deal with similar territory as in *The Road to Day-break*, but even more intimately, since this is Nouwen's account of working with a profoundly disabled epileptic while living in L'Arche Daybreak in Toronto. Before I comment further on this work, let me clarify that rather than speak to portions of this work and make a comment based on every quote, I want to pull a series of quotes, which I will address with one central theme. This story is at once beautiful and poignant, as well as somewhat disturbing and troubling. To tell the story of Adam, Nouwen uses the story of Christ and parallels Adam's journey of a brief and difficult life with epilepsy to Christ's ministry and difficult road here on earth. Although Nouwen attempts to make it very clear very early on that he is not trying to make Adam into Jesus, he straddles that line so closely throughout the book that the line almost completely disappears more than a few times. For example, beginning in the introduction, Nouwen says:

> I recognized many parallels between the story of Jesus and the story of Adam. And I knew something else. I knew, in a very profound place, that Adam, in some mysterious way, had become an image of the living Christ for me just as Jesus, when he lived on the earth, was friend, teacher, and guide for his disciples.[7]

7. Nouwen, *Adam*, 15.

In the chapter "Adam's Passion," Nouwen compares the "suffering of Adam" with the suffering of Jesus: "Adam's whole life was passion, a life of suffering in which he underwent everything that was done for him, to him, with him, and around him. His was primarily the suffering of complete dependence on other people's actions and decisions."[8]

Nouwen comes very close to deifying the circumstances surrounding Adam's life through statements like, "Adam was, like all of us, a limited person, more limited than most, and unable to express himself in words. But he was also a whole person and a blessed man. In his weakness he became a unique instrument of God's grace. He became a revelation of Christ among us."[9]

It should be noted here that in a portion not included in this excerpt, Nouwen does begin by saying, "I am not saying that Adam was a second Jesus."[10] However, in my opinion, he goes on to say everything but, "Adam was a second Jesus." I am not suggesting that Nouwen engaged in any kind of heresy, but that while valuing Adam's human worth, he also places Adam in a role Adam did not choose for himself: that of an image of Christ. I think it is important to note that we are all indeed called to manifest the image of Christ in and through our lives. My difficulty with the way Nouwen describes Adam's situation has much more to do with the fact that Nouwen seems to indicate that Adam's manifestation of the image of Christ is almost exclusively a result of Adam's perceived suffering. Here again, we find ourselves returning to what was said above in regards to some of Vanier's writing. I am not worried or concerned about the fact that the image of Christ appears through Adam's suffering. I am concerned about giving that suffering the exclusive avenue to the development of a Christ-like quality in Adam's life. I think at end of the day, Nouwen would agree and perhaps even does state that it is Adam's very being in all of his humanity that helps to express his Christ-like quality.

8. Nouwen, *Adam*, 84.
9. Nouwen, *Adam*, 30.
10. Nouwen, *Adam*, 30.

So, what do these excerpts from *Adam: God's Beloved* tell us? First, it must be said that this was a man who was deeply loved by Henri Nouwen and for whom Nouwen should be and is eternally grateful. There is no doubt in my mind that Nouwen's life and heart were truly changed by his relationship with Adam. This is beyond dispute, and one of the hundreds of conversations I will have with Nouwen one day is how I am eternally grateful that he did not once mention the ways in which Adam will one day have an un-blemished, unbroken body. He mentions someone else's dream to this effect, but Nouwen, for the most part, stays very clear of this typically Evangelical language.

All this being said, so closely linking the life of Jesus to the individual personal struggles of one man does not do credit to that individual as much as it makes him a parody of real human physical existence, even if that person would not argue with being the subject of such an exercise. I am not saying that we cannot learn sometimes deep and intimate things about life with Christ through our fellow human beings. However, to make a one-to-one comparison as Nouwen seems to do is not just folly; it is harmful because it gives those that would come after him the permission to do the same thing.

As someone deeply committed to walking the road of disci-pleship with others, I feel that the process of daily struggle and vic-tory in life is critical to articulating one's own story in the Kingdom of God. This is true no matter how profound the disability. To have someone grant you Christ-like status because you exist implies that they don't have a full understanding of the daily road with all of its victories, struggles, and challenges that I believe makes up each and every individual's unique journey towards sanctification. Perhaps this train of thought will make more sense if I end this section by referring back to Nouwen's *The Road to Daybreak*.

In his journal, there is an entire contemplation revolving around a stained-glass window depicting the transfiguration of Jesus, in which Nouwen says, "I had a new sense of the transfigu-ration that took place on Mount Tabor: God's light bursting forth from the body of Jesus."[11] To only refer to the disabled through their poverty, brokenness, and vulnerability is to be one of the disciples experiencing the transfiguration and wanting to build a tent to stay in the moment. In order to be transfigured by anyone's life experience, but most particularly the disabled, we've got to leave the mountain. The magnificent part of the transfiguration is the journey it inspired when the disciples came down. The impact of the life experience of the disabled is what we do beyond our physical or developmental circumstance. Jesus didn't stay on the mountain. Don't build tents for us, either.

Stanley Hauerwas

For our final conversation in this section, we turn to the theologian who has probably said more to the "able-bodied world" on behalf of those with disabilities than anybody in the last forty years, sometimes with varying effectiveness and sensitivity to the needs of the disabled. This is Dr. Stanley Hauerwas. Hauerwas began his relationship with the disabled community when he visited a hospital where many people with intellectual disabilities were kept during his time at the University of Notre Dame in the mid-1970s. The relationships he formed after his initial visit to the hospital led to his involvement in the Association for Retarded Citizens, and he eventually wrote numerous books and articles on the subject of individuals with disabilities. Dr. Hauerwas must be given remarkable credit for his advocating on behalf of the disabled long before it became a fashionable academic pursuit or even a recognized theological discipline. He does not take the normal path in advocating for the disabled that most who would identify themselves as disability theologians have taken. According to John Swinton:

> The goals of autonomy, rights, independence, equality, power, and freedom are precisely the types of social goods that are not available to people with such disabilities. Not only can they not access the political system in

11. Nouwen, *Road to Daybreak*, 142.

order to participate in change; they are also deeply vulnerable to that system.[12]

It seems to be Hauerwas's overwhelming conviction that it
is the role of the people of God to help the disabled discover their
identity within the Kingdom of God juxtaposed over and against
modernity because the disabled, particularly those with mental
or developmental disabilities, are not capable of articulating their
own story. Hauerwas, along with other theologians such as Hans
Reinders, is, in fact, very suspicious of what he describes as the
culture built on modern political theory. Hauerwas's skepticism
stems largely from systems where people are free to define themselves as they choose, provided they use the resources they are
given responsibly and give others the opportunity to participate
equally in the political and social processes. To use one of Hauerwas's favorite quotes, "[W]e live in a time when people believe they
have no story except the story they chose when they thought they
had no story."[13]

I have even heard Dr. Hauerwas say during a talk that it is
the church's responsibility to help the disabled tell their story because they are not fully capable of articulating their own story on
their own behalf. Let me say initially that I believe Dr. Hauerwas's
critique of modern political theory is very prescient and well-
constructed in many aspects. He is right to point out the dangers
of a society based largely on individual freedoms and autonomy
for those who do not conform to social norms. For example, many
individuals who do not communicate in normative ways or em-
body an alternative cognitive state could find themselves stripped
of dignity simply because they do not function within society's
definition of a free and autonomous individual.

As I will show as I continue in this section, difficulties begin
to arise in Hauerwas's treatment of the disabled when one begins
to notice that the argument that Hauerwas was making on behalf
of the disabled in the mid-1970s is the same argument he is still

12. Swinton, "Importance of Being a Creature," 512.
13. Hauerwas, "The Politics of Gentleness," Kindle edition, location 636.

making today with much the same language. I hope to demonstrate that no matter how well-intentioned or well-informed an argument, it must evolve with the people on whose behalf it is being made, and if the person making the argument refuses to evolve, he or she should not be given primacy within the intellectual discourse purely because they were the first to make the argument. In fact, when an individual's contribution on behalf of a disenfranchised group does not change for over forty years, what began as a noble and beneficial struggle can become dangerously outdated and as destructive as it was once constructive.

Let us begin our conversation by examining Hauerwas's essay "Community and Diversity: The Tyranny of Normality."[14] Although this essay was first published in 1986, it began as a speech given in 1977. This fact will become important a little later when we draw out one particular aspect of the language used by Dr. Hauerwas. What one notices first of all has to do with the basic premise of this essay, which is that he seeks to undermine the principle of "normality" by showing that true community respects diversity and difference. However, there is one small flaw: over and over in the essay, Hauerwas slips back and forth between advocating for difference and using an "us" and "them" construct to describe "normal" parents and their "retarded" children. We see this clearly in the following passage:

> Many talks about the retarded are about what we should be doing for them, but I am suggesting that they do something for us that we have hardly noticed. Namely, they force us to recognize that we are involved in a community life that is richer than our official explanations and theories give us the skill to say.[15]

The "us" and "them" language deployed in this passage is all the more stark because just prior to this paragraph, Hauerwas talks about the deep sense of commitment that helps demonstrate that the "retarded" move us toward "a community that enhances

14. Hauerwas, "Community and Diversity," 37–44.
15. Hauerwas, "Community and Diversity," 39.

us all." I don't need to point out that referring to "a community that enhances us all" using "us" and "them" language is silly, to say the least.

Later in this essay, we see Hauerwas engaging in a practice that we have already discussed in the context of both Jean Vanier and Henri Nouwen. In the section where Hauerwas describes what the "retarded" bring to their communities through how they handle their limits, he lists off several things:

> First, they have required their parents to join together and come in contact with others who are as different from them as their own children . . . Secondly, parents of retarded children discover what the world is like through their children . . . I have noticed the parents of retarded children know a lot more about politics than most of us . . . Finally, one of the things your children have done for you is to help you be free from the tyranny of the professional . . . what parents of retarded children learn to do is trust their own good judgment.[16]

Within each of these points, Hauerwas offers some detailed explanation of why it is an important issue. However, at no time during his explanation does he account for the fact that all of his ideas about what the "retarded" bring to a community have to do more with their parents than with themselves. Once again, we see an example of those with disabilities not so much developing their own identity as acting as a filter through which the nondisabled discover important life lessons. As we move forward, bear in mind that we will continue to see instances where Hauerwas's language is inconsistent at best.

Let me briefly make note of one glaring aspect of Dr. Hauerwas's writing that I think will demonstrate the inconsistency to which I refer, which is his rampant use of the word "retarded." In the research I have done, which is admittedly not exhaustive, but still very comprehensive, I see examples of Hauerwas using the words "mentally retarded" as late as 1986. While it can be reasonably assumed that it may take as much as ten to fifteen years or

16. Hauerwas, "Community and Diversity," 41–42.

perhaps longer for productive social change to take place on any deep or noticeable scale within popular culture, the fact that an academic of such renown was using the terminology "mentally retarded" as late as he was is inexcusable. Even as late as 2004 I have seen Dr. Hauerwas refer to the developmentally challenged as the "mentally handicapped." Although this term has much less virulent connotations than the word "retarded," it is still extremely outdated and has largely fallen out of use as a descriptor of those individuals with special needs.

As a person who deals with the constant variety presented in life due to my Cerebral Palsy, one of the things that strikes me immediately about Dr. Hauerwas's writings is the level of presumption that seems to exist within his writings. Take, for example, the paragraph found in the essay, "Suffering the Retarded: Should We Prevent Retardation?": "That such fellow-feeling is possible does not mean that they are 'really just like us.' They are not. They do not have the same joys we have nor do they suffer just as we suffer."[17] One can only imagine how statements like this would sound in the ears of parents and loved ones of those with physical and developmental disabilities, such as Joan, mother of Jimmy Hendrix and also a member of The Julian Way. Here again, we have an example where an "us" and "them" dynamic undermines any positive energy or intention that Hauerwas might have had in the statement in the first place. What bothers me the most about this particular passage, however, is the fact that there is a presumption that he knows how those with mental and developmental challenges feel or what type of emotion they are able to experience. This type of language is not just wrong; it is dangerous, no matter the purpose of the original statement. The minute I think I know what another person is feeling, I assume I have the right to think I know how best to handle "them." History is full of the devastating consequences of small statements like this.

Finally, through an examination of the essay "Timeful Friends," we come to what I view as the centerpiece of Hauerwas's ethics in regards to the disabled over and against current culture.

17. Hauerwas, "Suffering the Retarded," 103.

We see him in dialogue with Professor Michael Bérubé through Bérubé's book *Life as We Know It: A Father, a Family, and an Exceptional Child*. In it, Bérubé says, "I have no sweeter dream than to imagine—aesthetically and ethically and parentally—that Jamie will someday be his own advocate, his own author, his own best representative."[18] Hauerwas seems to think that it is sad and a consequence of the Bérubés being caught up in modernist humanism that causes Bérubé to see nothing but a future where Jamie is his own autonomous advocate. He juxtaposes what he believes to be Bérubé's position with his own by saying, "Dependency, not autonomy, is one of the ontological characteristics of our lives. That we are creatures, moreover, is but a reminder that we are created for and with one another. We are not just accidentally communal, but we are such by necessity."[19]

I whole-heartedly agree with Hauerwas's assertion that dependency is indeed an ontological characteristic of all humanity everywhere, and I am discovering more and more every day that the necessity of community is what builds God's Kingdom. Make no mistake about it, friends: without this fact, the previous 60 pages are meaningless. Where Professor Hauerwas and I would differ, however, is in this: he seems to be so committed to reacting against the general culture as to reject anything that even smells remotely like freedom and autonomy. I do not have quite the level of pessimism when it comes to freedom, autonomy, and self-definition. Let me explain.

When you are part of a culture that has been told who they are and what they are capable of for over one hundred years, discovering that you have a unique identity and quality of personhood within God's Kingdom is a completely liberating experience. I agree that completely unchecked, rampant individualism is not desirable in the least, but that is not what I am talking about here. Oftentimes, as we discover who we are in God's Kingdom, we begin with simply discovering who we are. That is the freedom I seek for my people through God's Community and in God's hands.

18. Bérubé, *Life as We Know It*, 264.

19. Hauerwas, "Timeful Friends," 16.

It might be understood that the type of individuality I am making reference to as a man proud of his Cerebral Palsy might not be at odds with Hauerwas's critique of the individualism of our modern culture. However, I would argue that as a people who, for such an extended period of time, were robbed of individuality and autonomy, the disabled interacting with modern culture and modern conceptions of individuality and autonomy is not entirely a bad thing, but rather a natural part of a people discovering their own voice and place in the larger world. Therefore, to always be so overtly critical and dismissive of individuality, as I believe Hauerwas is, is not to fully understand the place of a people who are reacting against a history of oppression and denial of their God-given selfhood.

I would never in my life want to completely deny or denigrate the work of someone as important as Stanley Hauerwas. In many ways, he was a voice for those with intellectual and developmental struggles before anyone else. But people with physical and developmental challenges are people in time, and in order to speak for them, we must know that times, circumstances, and conversations change. Whether it is Dr. Hauerwas's insistent battle with the windmills of modernity or his tragically out-of-date descriptions of the people for whom he claims to advocate, he shows symptoms of being someone who has become so wedded to a certain framework and idea set that he either cannot or refuses to change. As long as he is able to speak and bring ideas to the table, I would not seek to deny Dr. Hauerwas his distinguished seat at the conversational table, but we, as the disabled and those who care for them, must find a new primary voice—one that is able to fully recognize the freedom and full identity to which God is leading his people. Only then will the Red Sea once again fully part.

Excursus:
Reflections on My Journey through This Chapter

I would like to take a moment to share a brief reflection on what it has been like to journey with these three persons in particular, and most especially with Jean Vanier, through the writing process. I am well acquainted now with the literary peril that can often come from engaging critically with persons who are still living, or whose writing still holds such a prominent position within the broader culture, such as Henri Nouwen, especially persons who have done so much to invest in and enhance the spiritual and physical well-being of so many. During the course of this writing process, some whom I consider friends and colleagues have speculated as to whether I am too close to this particular section of this book to write from an objective perspective, and whether I am too critical of the three theologians we have just engaged. Let me first say that as an individual with a disability who largely awoke to the presence of disabled culture through the writing of this book, I do indeed have wounds and scars that I deal with every day from discovering how my people, that is, people with disabilities, have been treated in the not-too-distant past. But rather than be a hindrance to the great work of disability advocacy and theology, I hope that my wounds spur me on to treat all those I come into contact with, whether in person or through my writing, with a sense of charity, fairness, and understanding. For my part, I think Jean Vanier especially is to be commended because of his willingness to bring those with intellectual disabilities to the communal table of conversation when no one else would. He in many ways did more than any other Christian of the twentieth century to make the concerns of the intellectually disabled human concerns that should be shared by the whole Christian community. Similarly, Nouwen did as much to bring the concerns of the developmentally disabled to the attention of a broad popular audience as anyone has in the last forty years. His openness to community, and the brilliance of his writing and thought in the books mentioned above as well as others, offer a depth and complexity to the disabled experience that was largely previously unseen, particularly in Christian literature. I will admit, fully and openly, that I am a little bit harder on Stanley Hauerwas, because of his slowness to address inconsistencies in his language and thought, but even he must be applauded for introducing the situation of disability into academic discourse with a level of passion and intimacy rarely seen. I think each of these men would not begrudge the effort to move the work forward, however. If I am critical, I am critical because new paths are needed, new conversations must be had, and I am privileged as a person with a disability to be in a position to discover what's next, while never forgetting the groundwork laid by men like these who go before me.

5

The Old Is New Again

Looking at Community with
Julian of Norwich and Dietrich Bonhoeffer

As WE CONCLUDE THE theological explorations in this book, we end with two theologians from two different points in time: Julian of Norwich, a fourteenth-century British anchoress, and Dietrich Bonhoeffer, a twentieth-century Lutheran giant. Both Julian and Bonhoeffer help us turn the corner from theological ideas to the practical day-to-day reality of embodiment, and then to community.

Julian of Norwich

The woman known as Julian of Norwich was granted a series of startling visions during a serious illness in the year 1373. The intimacy and clarity of these visions paint a picture of a wounded, bleeding, and loving Savior that is most certainly different from any conception of Jesus ever laid down before this point, and perhaps Julian is beyond comparison throughout the history of Christian texts. As Amy Laura Hall expounds, Julian's text was the first text written by a woman in English, and that her gender is uniquely tied to her conception of Christ:

> Even if she was not a wife or a mother (and she may, for all we now know, have been both), she was raised by women in a society divided clearly along gender lines. This facet of her life is helpful to understand the form and content of her vision of Christ. Her gender and her life as a woman who cooked for kin, nursed infants, and cleaned wounds is intertwined with the revelation of Christ granted to her by God.[1]

Julian's visions offer unique perspective and opportunity for those with disabilities because of the way she speaks of the physicality of Christ within her visions. She has a way of discussing the beauty and God-given gift of embodied reality, as well as God's role in our creaturely existence, without denying the difficulty, pain, and often suffering that is that creaturely existence.

In Julian, I find someone who is able to say that God has both the first and the last word. It is Julian of Norwich that allows me to fully articulate my view of disability as a pure and lovely part of God's creation, rather than a rupture or disturbance of that creation. To understand how Julian allows me to make this claim, let us look at chapter 5 of *Revelations of Divine Love*, in which Julian says, "I saw which He is to us everything that is good and comfortable for us. He is our clothing that for love enwraps us, holds us, and all encloses us because of His tender love, so that He may never leave us. And so in this showing I saw that He is to us everything that is good, as I understood it."[2]

When one reads Julian, one must understand that in Julian's conception of creation, God (and therefore Jesus Christ) is responsible for absolutely everything created, and that God's love is such that everything created is absolutely and utterly good. Therefore, when she says things like, "He is our clothing that for love enwraps us, holds us, and all encloses us because of His tender love, so that He may never leave us," I believe that Julian is making a statement

1. Hall, "A Ravishing and Restful Sight," 156.
2. Julian of Norwich, *Revelation*, 77.

that God is so intimately involved and connected to his creation that he infuses all embodied reality with his love, grace, and Holy Spirit, even those forms of embodiment that others in God's creation would see as broken, fractured, or amiss.

Later, in this same chapter, Julian receives the vision of all of God's creation in the form of a hazelnut:

> Also in this revelation He showed me a little thing, the size of a hazel nut in the palm of my hand, and it was as round as a ball. I looked at it with the eye of my understanding and thought "What can this be?" And it was generally answered thus: "It is all that is made." I marveled how it could continue, because it seemed to me it could suddenly have sunk into nothingness because of its littleness. And I was answered in my understanding: "It continueth and always shall, because God loveth it; and in this way everything hath its being by the love of God. In this little thing I saw three characteristics: the first is that God made it, the second is that God loves it, the third, that God keeps it.[3]

It is through this vision of the hazelnut that is all of God's creation that I think we come to the first point at which Julian's theology can be radically transformative for those within the disabled culture. Julian's vision speaks directly in opposition to our current culture of hyper-individualism and the dramatic overemphasis on the perfect physical specimen as the ideal human embodiment. This is accomplished through Julian's utter simplicity. The vision of the entirety of God's cosmos—everything that is created—wrapped up in an object that fits in the palm of Julian's hand, shakes us from our overwhelming instinct to be the center of our own universe.

This is not to minimize any one individual's physical experience of embodied existence. However, Julian's vision can serve as a gentle but insistent reminder to those in the disabled culture that physical existence is not all there is. As an individual who deals with the demands and challenges of Cerebral Palsy—which include, but are not limited to: "Will I make it to the bathroom

3. Ibid.

on time this time?," "Is the arthritis in my hands and hips going to flare up at the next cold front?," and "Will the waitress at the restaurant ever speak to me at a normal volume?—it can be very tempting to live every day as though triumphing over my physical reality is the greatest thing I can do. When I think about Julian's hazelnut, I am given a context for my own existence and the fact that, no matter what my body may be experiencing that day, I am still a part of a universe in the palm of God's hand.

Julian's revelations offer answers and consolation in another long-standing issue within theology of disability. Throughout much of the history of Christianity, as far back as even the New Testament, it has been debated whether or not disability is a direct consequence of sin or even the manifestation of sin itself. Through examining Julian's parable of a servant and his lord and using the work of Amy Laura Hall to help explicate her view of fall and redemption, I hope to demonstrate that the tension between disability as suffering and physical or divine gift of God and example of God's creativity is a false dichotomy. In fact, Julian shows us that both of these realities can co-exist without diminishing the goodness of God's created world. First the parable:

> And then our kind Lord answered by showing in very mysterious images a wonderful parable of a lord who has a servant, and he gave me sight to aid my understanding of both . . . The lord sits with dignity, in rest and peace: the servant stands, waiting reverently in front of his lord, ready to do his will. The lord looks at his servant lovingly and kindly, and he gently sends him to a certain place to do his will. The servant does not just walk, but leaps forward and runs in great haste, in loving anxiety to do his lord's will. And he falls immediately into a slough and is very badly hurt. And then he groans and moans and wails and writhes, but he cannot get up or help himself in any way. And in all this I saw that his greatest trouble was lack of help; for he could not turn his face to look at his loving lord, who was very close to him and who is the source of all help.[4]

4. Hall, "A Ravishing and Restful Sight," 161.

Hall goes on to explain the parable:

> Is the servant the same earth creature who followed the
> serpent's lead? How could it be that God would grant as
> clarity such a story to describe the Fall, given that the
> servant is described as waiting, *ready to do his will?* In an
> extensive meditation on this vision, Julian discovers that
> both Adam and Christ have been united in the person of
> the servant; the suffering of Adam's fall and Christ's duti-
> ful suffering become so mixed as to be undistinguishable.
> "And thus our good Lord Jesus has taken upon himself
> all our guilt; and therefore our Father neither may nor
> will assign us any more guilt than he does to his own son,
> dearly loved Christ" (LT, 51). By Julian's vision the *imago
> Dei*, the fall of Adam, and sin and suffering are seen
> through the prism of the collapsed, salvific moment that
> is Christ. The doctrines are bled together in the bleeding
> of the new Adam. In this way, she comes to realize how
> "wretched sin" is, truly, *nothing.*[5]

Both Julian's vision and Hall's conception of that vision offer
the disabled an opportunity to reframe our place in the Christian
experience and the theological conversation. Through the parable
of the servant, we are shown an image of a servant in which is
blended, through the salvific work of the cross, the sacrifice of Jesus the Christ and the suffering of Adam. I believe if we take this
parable, look at it as a temporal collapse between the first Adam
and Jesus as the second Adam, and focus specifically on disability,
we see several things occur.

First, disability is removed from the realm of being exclusively a consequence of the Fall of man and is placed rather in the
category of another part of God's good creation that was corrupted
or damaged by sin. This, then, allows us to see people with disabilities playing roles in God's creation other than just exclusively
the victims of the sin-Fall narrative. To put it another way, perhaps
more colloquially, I like the image of "disabled creation" playing a
role in the Fall other than victim.

5. Ibid.

In the salvific moment on the cross, the servant in the form of the embodied Christ doesn't play the role of liberating those with so-called disabilities from their disabled bodies; rather, the servant helps those bodies rediscover their fullness in God's creation and experience the complete prism of their unique bodies beyond the fractured mirror of "disability."

To conclude our exploration of *Revelations of Divine Love*, we will now turn to chapter 12, in which Julian has a vision of the scourged body of Christ that seems to be drenched in his blood, which is surrounding her: "And this blood looked so plenteous that it seemed to me, if it had been as plenteous in nature and in matter during that time, it would have made the bed all bloody and have overflowed around the outside."[6] One can hardly imagine the potential bombshell that this phrase was to fourteenth-century ears. In a world surrounded by disease and constant threat of infection and death, to speak so familiarly of blood must have been evocative, to say the very least. That is precisely what we are after here. Julian liberates the body of Christ and Christ's healing blood from a medieval context that bound the blood of Christ in forms and rituals. This unbounded body of Christ is open to all and desperately yearns to be familiar with all. I can't help but reflect on the reality that so much of the stigma surrounding the disabled has to do with the unboundedness of our bodies. Let me see if I can explain.

It is an ever-present part of my reality to have to negotiate when, where, and how I will use the restroom when I am out in public. Most of the time, I have worked out systems wherein I can use the restroom before I leave the house and/or train my body to hold it until the appropriate moment when I return. However, not infrequently, I am confronted with the day-changing and plan-altering reality of a public bowel movement and/or lost race to the urinal. I know that there are many individuals with disabilities who deal with more dramatic public intrusions than I do. It is at these moments when our bodies become unaccommodating to public boundaries that being disabled moves from an abstract

6. Julian of Norwich, *Revelation*, 105.

conversation of social barriers to a real physical discussion of unruly and socially unacceptable bodies. When I see the Christ of Julian's vision violating every social boundary of her day and leaking his unbounded salvific blood all over the place, I know that boundaries no longer exist for me either, and I cease to be a creature bounded by appropriate or inappropriate behaviors. What if the blood of Christ and Eucharist itself became an unbounded, unwieldy instrument of salvation for all people?

Julian's theology is vital to the kingdom of God and to the community that will spring from this project because it takes, as its platform, a Christ for all embodied experience—not one that tries to minimize or ignore disability or play it into the alternate ultimate reality. Rather, Julian speaks to all existence, whether we call it nondisabled, disabled, normal, or other, and says, "Come, exist, and be yourself as God made you to be in the loving arms of our Mother Jesus."

Dietrich Bonhoeffer

Moving now to Dietrich Bonhoeffer, we will examine a theologian of superior intellect whose down-to-earth, realistic style is a guide for all people to learn to love, live, and worship as one community.

Bonhoeffer is probably best known for his vocal and courageous opposition to the Nazis and to the Nazi ideology of power and strength that threatened to overwhelm Germany and the world throughout the terrifying reign of the Third Reich. In Dietrich Bonhoeffer we see a theologian who speaks and lives as though the power of Christ is an active and firm reality in our daily world and for whom Christian community was a calling firmly rooted in the joy and pain, laughter and sorrow of daily living. In our examination of Bonhoeffer we will begin by taking a look at some of the writings in which Bonhoeffer directly addresses the situation of people with disabilities in Nazi Germany. We will spend the bulk our time looking at *Life Together,* Bonhoeffer's masterpiece regarding intentional Christian community and the way that Christians are called to live together in true fellowship. We will use

Life Together as a bridge point between the theological investigations that make up the first half of this book and the narrative that will begin to envision the community that my wife, Lisa, and I feel called to live into.

Beginning in 1933, with the ascension of Adolf Hitler as the Chancellor and Führer of the German people, Germany began its decent into a policy of isolation, discrimination, and eventually murder of those populations it would deem as less than desirable or genetically inferior. The sad reality is that many Christians in Germany were either knowingly or unknowingly coopted or complicit in Germany's descent towards Nazi madness. The nationalistic fervor blinded many in Germany to the true evil behind Hitler's policies. Dietrich Bonhoeffer was never fooled and, indeed, was one of the earliest outspoken critics of the Nazi regime. In the 1934 sermon given in London dealing with the place of weakness in our world, Bonhoeffer calls his flock to take a stand of intellectual honesty and moral fortitude toward those who are perceived as weak in the world when he says, "we feel it somewhat dangerous to give account of our fundamental attitude. But God does not want us to put our head into the sand like ostriches, but he commands us to face reality as it is and to make a truthful and definite decision."[7] In this call to action Bonhoeffer is displaying both the realism and practicality that has endeared him to millions of people throughout the years and the courage and foresight that would eventually lead to his death in 1945 at the hands of the Nazis.

Although he uses language that would seem to echo some other theologians examined in this project in the way he seems to make disability synonymous with sickness, weakness, and the unfortunate, I believe that Bonhoeffer would say that on balance, creaturely existence is best lived out when one takes into account the whole of that existence. Bonhoeffer does not seem so much to prize health over sickness or strength over weakness as much as he says it is all part of creaturely existence. He makes this point clearly in his *Ethics* when he writes, "Both the flourishing of life's strength and self-denial, growth and death, health and suffering,

---

7. Bonhoeffer, "Sermon for the Evening Worship," 372–74.

happiness and renunciation, achievement and humility, honor and self-deprecation belong inextricably together in a living unity full of unresolved contradictions."[8] The paradoxical balance that Bonhoeffer strikes in statements like this is what makes him an ideal conversation partner as we look towards an intentional faith community involving both the disabled and nondisabled. To conclude this section, we will examine *Life Together* to see in what ways the people of God might be being called into further love in the world and to engagement with one another.

As my wife and I think and pray about this community, one of the many aspects that keeps emerging in our minds is the various and diverse forms of disabled experience that exist in the world today. As has already been stated in this book on a number of occasions, trying to narrow down the experience of disability using one or two marks or indicators is nearly impossible. In fact, it is not an altogether rare experience that when I am with others in the disabled community, I begin to notice a sort of competition developing about whose experience of suffering is most acute and who has the most right to hold on to resentment and persecution. I will be the first to admit that when I have the opportunity to get together with a number of people with Cerebral Palsy within a larger disabled group, I tend to gravitate towards those with Cerebral Palsy because of our common experience and pride in our situation. Rivalry between various disabled groups could and does make real, genuine community a very difficult thing to achieve. Bonhoeffer speaks the Holy Spirit's word into this situation, when in *Life Together* he says,

> A Christian comes to others only through Jesus Christ. Among men there is strife. "He is our peace," says Paul of Jesus Christ (Eph. 2:14). Without Christ there is discord between God and man and between man and man. Christ became the Mediator and made peace with God and among men . . . Only in Jesus Christ are we one, only

8. Bonhoeffer, "*Ethics:* Christ, true man," 387–89.

through him are we bound together. To eternity he remains the one Mediator.[9]

In a very real sense, Bonhoeffer helps the disabled community have a conversation that I feel is needed in a bad way. For
those in the disabled community to claim their rightful place in
community with one another and in the larger theological and cultural conversation, it is not necessary that we abandon our pride
in our unique disabled situations, but disability can no longer be
the starting point and the centerpiece of our reality. We must allow Christ to be the beginning and ending of our conversation.
Then disability can become one note in God's song of harmony
and peace instead of a screaming, shrill voice that drowns out all
others.

Bonhoeffer's *Life Together* can help us find a path toward true
Christian community, not only within the disabled community,
but also in the disabled culture's approaches to the nondisabled
world and its interaction with nondisabled individuals. It may be
difficult to hear from one who has spent seventy-plus pages advocating for a more open, integrated view of those with disabilities
within the larger Church and theological world, but I believe we,
in the disabled community, do have a tendency to be rather in-
sular towards the larger world. It's important to stop and keep in
mind that this frequent tendency toward insularity may best be
described as a response to wounds or trauma rather than a straight
desire to form an isolated, separated community. There are too
many instances to mention where those with disabilities have
come to the table looking for a fair shake and been harmed in the
process, whether intentionally or unintentionally. This has caused
over the years those with disabilities to operate from a posture of
suspicion, doubt, and downright hostility when conversing with
anyone who is nondisabled, or worse, does not openly choose to
identify as disabled.

My wife and I want the community that we begin to be a place
of righteousness expressed through gentleness and reconciliation.

---

9. Bonhoeffer, *Life Together*, Kindle edition, location 121.

For this to occur, we must take Bonhoeffer's words to heart, when he speaks of this righteousness by saying,

> [The redeeming Word] can come only from the outside. In himself he is destitute and dead. Help must come from the outside, and it has come and comes daily and anew in the Word of Jesus Christ, bringing redemption, righteousness, innocence, and blessedness.[10]

Innocence in this quote is very intriguing for me. For too long the word innocence, when connected to the disabled, has seemed to refer to some innate quality that the disabled possess over and against the rest of the world. The innocence that Bonhoeffer talks about being restored when we look outward through Christ and Christ's Word is innocence that is found in Jesus when we recognize that all parties, whether they be disabled or nondisabled, bear some responsibility and guilt for allowing the conversation to take place using a framework of hostility. When all God's creatures seek community in the Kingdom of God, we are no longer talking about innocence as something that is cheaply given based on one's physical or developmental circumstance. Rather, we are talking about innocence as a consequence of being a newly reconciled and continuously healing community of God's Kingdom. This is the innocence that truly fosters world-changing and life-changing conversations and consequences.

At the point at which this community was first being envisioned, I had a conversation with a colleague in the United Methodist Church in which it was asked, "What's to stop you from creating a disabled ghetto of love, and isolating yourself?" This is an understandable concern. As we have already noted several times in this section, this is a community within the disabled context, but even to only speak of this community in such terms is selling it short somewhat. For this place to be a vision of God's Kingdom, it's got to be a vision for all, regardless of their circumstance. I think

---

10. Bonhoeffer, *Life Together*, Kindle edition, location 106.

this is accomplished primarily by keeping in mind the difference between what Bonhoeffer calls "spiritual love" and "human love."[11]

If we are to build a community for all, it must be a community where all can both give and receive love and give and receive service. We must love and serve to glorify Christ. We cannot love and serve merely because we want to love and serve other people. If we come to community to find Christ by interacting with those with disabilities or by "allowing" the nondisabled to serve the disabled, we will inevitably attach ourselves to the individuals we serve, and to those who serve us. This is human love. Spiritual love calls both the nondisabled and disabled, regardless of where they find themselves or whether they find themselves serving or being served, to serve Christ. That is the only way to avoid the attachment that, according to Bonhoeffer, kills real community.

If I might take even a little bit more license, human love has taken us quite far in the conversation within the disabled community, but the end of the road for human love is inclusion. The end of the road for spiritual love is Jesus Christ, when we have moved from inclusion to the mutually reconciling and empowering reality of the Kingdom of God.

As we close this section on Dietrich Bonhoeffer and this larger look at the theology of the church within this book, I am reminded that the process that my wife and I are on towards the opening of this community is a process that belongs squarely to God, and the healing and peace that will be a result of the community by God's grace is God's responsibility as well. As this project has come to define what will in many ways be the great work of my life as a pastor of Jesus Christ, my darling wife and I have had many conversations in which I felt the heaviest weight of my life when it comes to bearing the ultimate responsibility for this endeavor. It is for that reason and for anyone else who would ask me why this community is important and would wonder whether or not it's unnecessary that I include this last Bonhoeffer quote:

11. See Bonhoeffer, *Life Together*, Kindle edition, location 215.

Christian community is like the Christian's sanctification. It is a gift of God which we cannot claim. Only
God knows the real state of our fellowship, of our sanctification. What may appear weak and trifling to us may
appear great and glorious to God. Just as the Christian
should not be constantly feeling his spiritual pulse, so,
too, the Christian community has not been given to us
by God for us to be constantly taking its temperature.[12]

This quote reminds me that, just as sanctification in the life
of the Christian is a continuous and life-long journey, the journey
towards this community and a Kingdom-based understanding
between the disabled and nondisabled is a long process, one that I
can only trust to the ever-loving hands of God. Therefore, we move
forward with the conviction that God's diversity and imagination
is deeper and more complex than humans can imagine. Within
that imagination, embodiments that have previously been seen as
broken are truly expressions of God's first and last word of divine
creativity, co-participants in life with God and all creation. Hence,
the project of The Julian Way, as illustrated in the following section, is a radical call to life with God in mutual interdependence
with one another as all persons, disabled and nondisabled, discover and express their own stories in the great narrative of God's
love for the world.

12. Bonhoeffer, *Life Together*, Kindle edition, location 208.

PART II

A Community Story

Cast of Characters (in order of appearance)

Daniel—A man with vision impairment in his mid-to-late 30s who is married to Sarah

Sarah—An able-bodied woman in her mid-to-late 30s who is married to Daniel

Alex—A young man in a wheelchair, mid-20s, living with spina bifida

Carolyn—A single, able-bodied female community member in her 50s or 60s

Russell Hendrix—12-year-old able-bodied twin brother of Jimmy

Jimmy Hendrix—12-year-old boy with Cerebral Palsy

Joan Hedrix—able-bodied mother of twins Russell and Jimmy in her late 30s or early 40s, wife of Tommy

Tommy Hendrix—able-bodied father of twins Russell and Jimmy, in his mid-40s, husband of Joan

Lisa—able-bodied woman in her early 30s, wife of Justin

Justin—mid-30s, living with Cerebral Palsy, husband of Lisa

Karen Clark—able-bodied neighbor and friend of The Julian Way in her mid-to-late 60s, wife of Steve

Steve Clark—neighbor and friend of the Julian Way, in his mid-to-late 60s, deals with Parkinson's, husband of Karen

Adam—able-bodied graduate student in his late 20s studying universal design

In Part II we will switch gears by narratively exploring what a community like The Julian Way might look like by examining several different events in the life of the community. I will paint a picture of the type of place of peace and healing we hope to develop at The Julian Way by taking us on a narrative tour to observe several key events in the life of the community. As we enter the story of community together, we will imagine the life rhythms of how a variety of people with different physical embodiments live and move together within the daily flow of community life. Throughout this story, we will meet a recurring group of residents of The Julian Way as well as friends and neighbors. In order to allow you to engage as quickly and deeply as possible, I have included at the beginning of this chapter a list of the people you will meet as we journey through this look at life in The Julian House.

Family Dinner

We are standing in a large open kitchen with much joy and laughter filling the air along with what smells like the delicious scent of roast chicken and turkey. Looking around the room we see Daniel and Sarah talking animatedly while preparing vegetables for a salad. The first thing we notice when we look closer at this situation is that both Daniel and Sarah are chopping vegetables, which might not be so strange until you realize that Daniel is blind. He is using a set of brightly colored knives that appear to have brail dots on the handle in order to indicate what type of knife is being used and where to position his hand. We see Sarah occasionally helping him by standing the vegetable or removing excess ingredients when the chopping is done and while she is watching carefully she is also participating in an animated discussion with Alex about the time Daniel tried to dye his hair in college. Instead of subtle red highlights, he ended up with an exploding maroon fiasco.

"Yes," Daniel says, "but everyone knew I was coming on campus and it got your attention enough that you asked me out."

"So, you think your maroon head was the reason I asked you out? I was merely trying to save you from anymore cosmetic decisions," laughed Sarah.

"Hey it worked out for me," says Daniel while finishing a pile of carrots.

Alex chimes in, "Maybe that is what I need, to dye my hair blue or get a nose ring." At that moment Carolyn laughs, "I think the nose ring might be a little much," as she and Alex prepare to pull the turkey out of the oven. As they open the French-door oven that's right on-level with his wheelchair, Alex says, "smells delicious" as his face disappears into the oven to look longingly at the turkey. Carolyn says, "Careful kid, I can't have you pulling a Hansel and Gretel and falling in. It does look splendid though." Carolyn places the rubber covering over Alex's legs so that he can help wheel the turkey to the table in the dining room.

At that moment we hear Russell Hendrix pipe up from the center of the kitchen where he is helping his brother and mother make bread dough on a large island, "Mom can I get an earring?" Jimmy his twin with Cerebral Palsy says, "Russell, that would be awesome! Can I be the one to pierce your ear? I promise that my hands will only be a little twitchy. You wouldn't mind a hole in the side of your head would you? Of course, what little brains you have might spill out!" Russell yells as a clump of dough flies across the table. At that moment mother, Joan, says, "That is enough boys! Jimmy you are not putting a hole in your brother's head. I don't even let your father hold sharp objects." Tommy yells from the living room, "Sure you can get an earring! As long as you also get a tattoo on your arm that says my mom calls me sweetums!" At that moment Jimmy bursts out laughing. Russell tries not to laugh while expressing twelve-year-old outrage. Joan from the kitchen replies, "You're helping dear, thank you."

As Joan and Russell continue to knead the dough for bread, Joan asks Jimmy to go get more flour from the cabinet. Jimmy rolls over, pulls the specially designed lever for the correct cabinet and the cabinet with the flour in it lowers down to allow Jimmy to reach inside and find the flour. As they slip the bread onto the top rack of the oven, Joan is thinking how fortunate they were to find this place through someone at their church. The family moved to Dallas six months ago and stayed in a hotel initially while looking for a house. The hotel got too expensive after a while, and they did not know what the next step was going to be. Finding an accessible apartment in the city that could comfortably accommodate their family and allow Jimmy the freedom to move around with as much independence as possible had proved very difficult. Then, a woman at the Methodist church where the family had been attending who had known Carolyn for several years told them about The Julian Way. She knew that The Julian Way was a community that tried the best it could to accommodate disabled families. So, the Hendrixes thought they would give it a try. They had been in the community for a little more than two months now and were still actively looking for a place to live. Although the boys had a little bit of trouble adjusting to the Rule of Life of the house at first, they liked the people, and Joan and Tommy were so glad to have made so many new friends in Dallas.

They waited a couple of hours to let everything finish cooking, during which time Justin and Lisa came in from shopping and helped the rest of the community set the table for dinner. Located just off the large kitchen, the table is a long sturdy wooden table with removable benches and chairs and plenty of space and height to accommodate chairs, walkers, and other mobility devices. As they sit down, both the boys begin yelling with joy trying to outdo each other, "You gotta try the bread, we made it!" At which point Daniel says, "I made the salad. Watch out for my finger," he said playful while holding down one of the fingers on his left hand. After praying a blessing over the meal, the community enjoyed dinner, a lively conversation, and many jokes and laughter. After dinner, Alex, Daniel, and the boys went to the living room to watch TV and play board games while Lisa, Justin, Carolyn, and the rest of the community commenced with cleaning the kitchen. As Justin and Tommy pushed the island to the corner of the kitchen so that Justin could mop and Tommy could clean the island, Justin asked, "How are you all liking it here?"

"Oh it is great for the most part," Tommy said.

"Good, is there anything that is difficult or not what you imagined?" Justin said with a friendly smile.

"No," Tommy said while reaching for a bottle of cleaner. "It's just been somewhat interesting to try to explain to the boys what a Rule of Life is and why this community does what it does, especially because neither Joan nor I have much experience with that. We've basically been mainline Methodists all of our lives. I did have a little Pentecostal experience in my youth, but even that is different from living in community," Tommy said.

"And how are those conversations going?" Justin asked while adjusting the mop in his hand.

"Pretty good I guess. We are just trying to tell the boys that the things you all do, the Rule of Life around here, is a way for the community to constantly be connected to the Holy Spirit and working to be better Christians," Tommy replies.

"Good answer," Justin says as he finishes his final pass with the mop. "The Rule of Life, the prayers, presence, gifts, service, and witness that we talk about at The Julian Way is also a way that we are kind to our neighbors, like the Clarks across the street. You met them last Saturday. The need in their lives that we noticed right off the bat is help getting to the store because it is not easy for them to drive. The Rule of Life helps us to notice their desire for someone to care for them. That's why one of us tries to go over every day and make sure that things are still working in the house as it gets colder."

As they finish cleaning the kitchen and move to join the others in the living room, Tommy says, "I really like that caring for your neighbor is such an important part of what we have found here. It is just a little bit strange because we are so used to spending most of our energy navigating our own lives. We have always thought neighboring was more about being polite." At that moment Carolyn, who had been with the others in the living room, said, "I know. We have been here a couple of years and there are times when the Rule of Life seems strange. It's a bit like coming home after a long absence. You know it feels familiar and it is where you belong, but it takes a while to truly feel like home. The Rule of Life helps us feel home in God's call. No worries though, you are doing just fine."

The Sunday dinner episode helps us imagine an environment where everybody regardless of physical condition can move freely and with total access in a kitchen. Some of the things mentioned in this story, such as the cabinets that raise and lower and the knives equipped with brail, are ideas that we hope help give everybody the opportunity to engage in the creative process of God's hospitality. Come with me now as we look at another area of fruitful possibility for God's imagination within this community.

Time in the Garden

As we join The Julian Way again, the community is out for a day of gardening and fun in the soil. Joining them in this day of nature is their neighbor Karen Clark. The people of The Julian Way have been friends with Karen and her husband Steven for quite some time, and they often help the Clarks around their house and the community when Karen needs an extra hand caring for her husband who is living with Parkinson's disease. The community knows and loves the Clarks well, and Sarah and Daniel discovered that Karen has a green thumb, so The Julian Way has invited her to help in their garden whenever Steven is feeling well enough. Justin is taking Karen on a tour of their garden space when Karen notices how much room there is on the pathways in the garden and how interestingly everything is arranged. Karen says, "I can't believe that five people, two of them in wheelchairs, are able to work in one garden space." Justin replies, "Yes, we make sure that this space is arranged in such a way that the path ways are big enough to accommodate several chairs. We might not always need that much space, but it is good to know it is there. That way, everyone can participate."

As they move through the garden, Karen comments, "I remember what Daniel told me about the raised beds in the garden; about how they were they built with cut outs and space for chairs and now I see Alex is working in one." They stroll over to Alex, working in one of the raised beds. He is manipulating a pepper plant into position in a raised planting bed with a circular cut out in it that leaves him plenty of room to maneuver is his chair. Alex is also handling a trowel with an easy grip handle that allows him to hold the implement with as little strain as possible. They arrive at the bed just in time to hear Alex say, "Got it! Now pack in some dirt and a little bit of compost and she'll be ready to roll." They watched as Alex carefully scoops dirt around the plant along with natural compost from another bin at his station. Karen gives Alex a smile and says, "Great job. Couple weeks of warm weather and you'll begin to see some progress." Alex smiles mischievously and says, "I hope so, I have never really planted anything before. When I was a kid and could help my mom they nicknamed me the Black Thumb of Death due to my habit of killing things that grow." Lisa hears this and laughs from across the way saying, "We know. That is why we are giving your peppers a wide berth! Just in case old habits are hard to break." As she says this she walks over to say hi to Karen and says to Alex, "It really looks good though. I am quite impressed."

The three continue to walk around the garden and they join Joan and the Hendrix boys at a similar gardening table like the bed that Alex was at. Joan is watching the boys run their fingers through the dirt with a bemused yet delighted smile on her face. She says, "I never thought my boys were much for nature, but once I explained to them that mixing the manure and compost together needed to be done and also meant that they could get as dirty as they could possibly want, they went wild." "Squish" goes the pile of manure as Jimmy and Russell are mixing the bits of all the vegetables and manure together to create compost. "They look like they found their calling," Karen says.

Russell says, "You bet! Now if I can only convince Mom and Dad that we make better compost when we don't bathe, we'll be home free."

Their mother says, "That's not how it works Russell, sorry. But it does look like you guys are doing a great job. This stuff is really gonna help with the tomatoes and squash."

The journey continues to where Sarah and Carolyn are working in a plot of ground near some of the raised beds, but at ground level this time. Karen says, "So I guess this is the tomatoes and the squash?" Sarah says, "Yep, hopefully, with the boys' magic fertilizer, the squash will take this time."

Sarah asks Justin to assist her in breaking up some dirt with a tiller nearby. Justin grabs the tool and starts to work. Again, the tiller is designed with an extra-large easy-grip handle for individuals who have a difficult time grabbing gardening tools and has a special bearing on the bottom the makes the tiller easy to turn once it is in the soil.

As Sarah slides the tomato plant in place, Carolyn is also planting squash in a nearby area of the same space. Carolyn says, "Man, I do love squash. Now if they would only pop out of the ground the instant I put them in there we wouldn't have to wait.

From across the garden, Jimmy says, "And if they would only pop out of the ground with bread crumbs and cheese on them, that would be awesome as well."

Carolyn says, "I'll look for the casserole plants the next time I am at the nursery."

Justin, gesturing excitedly, says to Karen, "Let's continue, come over here I want to show you this." Lisa says, "Oh yes, he's so proud," as they walk up on yet another raised bed with working space. Justin gestures to what is unmistakably a rosemary plant and from out of a small circular cut out within the workspace attached to the bed, he pulls out a small water can. "I water these every day; they're my project. I'm also working on some basil in the other bed over there," he grandly points a few feet to the left.

Karen says, "Look at you developing a green thumb. I always knew you saw the need for a garden, but I never thought I'd see you so excited to be participating."

"Just trying to do my part," Justin says.

Lisa whispering conspiratorially to Karen says, "I haven't told him yet that we have given him the things that are next to impossible to kill. I'm letting him have his moment for now." Karen, Lisa, and Carolyn who overheard the conversation all start to laugh.

As they finish their way around the garden, they come to what looks like a large table located at the center of the garden with levers and buttons on it, as well as attachments for hoses which seem to be extending to all of the beds and planting spaces around the garden. Tommy is explaining to Daniel how each of the different hoses is connected to a lever button on the table. "We had a similar system at where I used to work before we came to The Julian Way. Hopefully this works the way we think it will, when you push down on the lever the hose will start. Try this one." Tommy guides Daniel to a particular lever with a handle textured with bumps. Daniel pushes down on the lever and the soaker hose in the bed with the pepper plants comes to life. Tommy says, "It worked! One for one!" He helps Daniel guide his hand to another lever with a ridged handle this time. "Now pull up on this one." Daniel does so and the hose near the tomatoes and squash comes on this time. They repeat the process several more times with each handle or lever having a different grip or texture so that Daniel is able to easily determine which hose was connected to which handle. Both Tommy and Daniel cheer and begin to dance. Simultaneously they say to their wives, "Look honey, we are doing the sprinkler!" to moans and groans all around.

Later, after the gardening is done, the community gathers inside and Karen brings Steven back for cake and coffee. Both of the Clarks remark how wonderful the garden is looking. Sarah and Lisa discuss with the Clarks why the garden is important to The Julian Way.

Lisa says, "We want to create a space that can eventually hold enough beds and gardening plots to feed not just ourselves but the neighborhood. It is going to take a while, but we are almost there."

Sarah adds, "And now that Tommy has helped us put the water table in we've taken one large step in that direction."

Steven says, "My wife was telling me about the way each bed is set up with spaces cut out for chairs and enough room for anybody to work with them."

Alex says, "Yes, Steven, I love working out there because it really lets me get my hands dirty, no pun intended, but I really have a role to play. Knowing that we will eat the peppers that I planted today and that you and your wife will enjoy them as well is something that means a lot to me."

Justin says, "We do want everybody to experience the feeling of being in relationship with God's earth. Our garden is designed such that regardless of who is living with us or what their physical situation is, every member of the community produces something, or at least has the option to produce something."

Daniel speaks up from the other end of the table, "There were times when I was younger when my vision difficulties made me feel like I was in a very small world. Working in the garden helps me realize, even if it is in small ways, that I am a part of God's larger creation. I am helping God create by planting vegetables for us to eat and feeding the neighborhood."

Tommy speaks up and says, "It's really helped the boys to think about what they eat on a daily basis and not just take for granted where their food comes from." Karen looks at the clock and notices it is almost time for another round of Steven's medications. Carolyn and Lisa leave with the Clarks to help them get Steven back to the house. Before they go, The Julian Way household invites the Clarks back for a day in the garden whenever they like. As they are walking out the door, Justin says, "We try to have a day where everybody is out in the garden planting at least once a month. Come back anytime and we may even put you and Steven to work next time." There are smiles and laughter all around as the evening comes to an end.

The scene in the garden is just one vision of what The Julian Way hopes to achieve by living in nature and interacting with creation in a responsible way. Lisa and I think it is critical that the local and universal church take responsibility for its witness to the earth and God's creation by creating a space where nondisabled and disabled individuals can work side by side to enhance the earth and grow natural healthy food. We create an environment that says as much about the fullness God wishes for all of creation as almost anything else we do.

Universal Design and The Julian Way

As we rejoin The Julian Way one last time, we find Justin and Lisa giving a tour of the house to Adam a student from the local community college who is doing a project on architecture and building for the disabled community. Adam joins Justin and Lisa at nine o'clock on a Saturday morning in the parking lot right next to the garden. Justin says, "Hey, Adam, I hope you didn't have any trouble finding the place."

"No, it was fairly easy," replies Adam. "In fact, it was part of my project. I am supposed to evaluate certain things about the surrounding area. I noticed that we are in the Oak Cliff area of Dallas and the DART buses and trains are within walking distance. Was that something you all paid attention to when you planned the community?"

Lisa replies with a polite smile, "Yes, that's a very nice catch. We think it's very important for all of our community members and friends to be acquainted with the city of Dallas, so we wanted to be close to public transit access points. In fact, we partner with a local attendant care and independent living agency to help coordinate public transit training classes every year or when someone new moves into the community."

Justin says, "Yes, we've even taught the Hendrix boys to be aware of public transit. It's another way we want The Julian Way community to feel like Dallas is their home rather than just a place they are staying or where they live."

Lisa says, "The rest of the community is out for breakfast and an afternoon at the movies today. If you can stay, they will join us later in the afternoon to answer questions. Let's go inside. There's coffee and snacks, and we'll show you some aspects of the house."

"Sounds great," replies Adam.

They walk through the parking lot, through the garden and up to the front door. When they arrive at the front door, Justin indicates to Adam that they should stop and look at something. "Can you tell me if you noticed anything while we were walking up?" asks Justin.

Adam says, "No, not really, other than the flower beds along the way."

Justin laughs and says, "That's another nice catch."

Adam replies, "What, the flower beds?" Lisa says, "It's not just about the flower beds. If you notice, the pathway does gently slope up like a ramp, but we are very big on creating an environment where any glaring indicators of accessibility flow into the natural environment. That's why, although there are handicap spots, there is not a clear indication of a ramp because we want every access point to be as level as possible for everybody. Even though the sidewalk slopes up like a ramp, we plant the garden around the ramp and the flowerbeds, so that you are walking through a beautiful garden space and not an obviously ramped accessible pathway."

At this point, Justin says with an air of playful impatience, "Yes, yes, but we are at the front door, can I show him the coolest part of the house?"

To which Lisa replies, "Gosh you guys and technology, you'd think you installed the thing yourself."

"Of course I didn't install it," Justin says, "it would have gone much faster if I had done it." At this point Adam gives the two of them a quizzical look, to which Lisa urges Justin, "Okay, show him, show him."

Justin says, "You can see that there are two pads on the side of the doorway here. One is at regulation standing height, right at about to where your arm is. Wave your hand in front of that pad." Adam did and the door swung open.

"Very cool," Adam says.

They let the door close and Lisa says, "Now, what if someone in a chair wants get through the door but cannot reach to wave at the sensor? Watch what Justin does."

Justin rolls up and gently taps his foot against the sensor mounted low on the door frame. The door opens just as it had before.

Justin says, "That way someone in a chair or standing can reach the door. We also have an audio capability so that a blind person knows where to put their hand or how to stand to open the door. That takes a little bit of training, but it works."

Adam says, "Yeah I've seen a similar thing on traffic lights around town."

Lisa says, "Yeah, of course, that is exactly what it is."

As they walk inside, Justin says, "We have a similar set up on every exterior door of the house. We are working on eventually having enough money to get visual recognition on the door so that someone who is paralyzed can most easily open the door independently. For now, when we have a friend who comes over here in that situation they use the foot control."

Lisa says as they enter the large living area, "We also have push button automatic doors on most of the interior, along with levered handles if nothing else is available." Justin says, "There is just one more thing about the doors, before we take you to see the living area and the rest of the house, you'll notice that none of the doors at The Julian House have thresholds. That's another part of universal architecture that we wanted to incorporate, so that it is as easy as possible for individuals with a wide range of disabilities to move in and out of the property."

They now stand in a large communal area with outlets spaced at even intervals at chair height along the wall. "Welcome to the great room," Lisa says. "You can see there's a TV over there and a fireplace along the other wall with plenty of room to stretch out."

Adam says, "This room is awesome."

To which Justin replies, "I know, I feel like a king in Lord of the Rings whenever I am in the room alone."

To which Lisa replies, "it is harmless to let you pretend."

Justin says, "Well, anyways, we want to show you this room because there is something here that makes a huge difference to accessibility and flow of the environment that most people don't think of. In fact, we didn't think of it until we were dreaming of this community. Can you guess what it is? You are the architecture student on a roll after all."

Adam pauses for a moment and thinks. "I'm not completely sure, but does it have something to do with the outlets and where they are placed?"

"Right on the money once again. We should call you when we want something designed," says Justin. "We placed the outlets around the room like this so that people with disabilities can easily plug things in and we could minimize tripping over equipment cords strung along the floor as much as possible. It's not perfect, but we think it works pretty well."

As they continue the tour, Lisa says, "If you'll notice, most of the light switches are in similar positions to the outlets for much of the same reason."

The tour moved into the large kitchen, where they demonstrated the cabinets that rotated up and down for easy access, along with the French-door oven and the mobile island. At which point Lisa says, "Okay, now it is time for my favorite part of the house, or what will be my favorite part of the house. We eventually will have a cooktop that has no oven underneath; that way individuals in chairs can roll up and place things on the cooktop and use it just as anyone else would." She glanced at Justin and said, "And then I'm going to teach this one to cook, slave away in the kitchen, and basically do whatever I ask."

Adam laughs and says, "It sounds like Justin is in for some work."

To which Lisa replies, "You betcha."

"Okay you two," Justin says, "we've got just enough time for a brief walk through of the family space before the others get back."

They move from the kitchen across the house into what appears to be a small sitting area and a bedroom. "This is our living area," says Justin, "as you can see we have a small area for relaxation and then our bedroom and bathroom. There are two more of these spaces around the house, along with two smaller guest rooms. It is a lot of space and it took a lot of time, but we live in community here, yet we also understand that we live with people who occasionally need their privacy. So, we try to provide that as best as we can. Within every room we have lights along the top of the wall for signaling to those with hearing impairments that community events are about to begin. You can see that ours is just above the sofa over there." Lisa says, "Our intention is that every event comes with a specific color. Yellow for house meeting, purple for prayer, along with colors for breakfast, lunch, and dinner."

Just then they hear a commotion as the rest of the community returns from their day out. As they walk back into the great room and find the Hendrix boys, Justin says, "Hey boys, how was the movie?" He is answered with a chorus of both of the boys yelling at once, "It was awesome! I love the Hunger Games!" Justin and Lisa introduce Adam to the boys as the rest of the community begins to gather around the table. Within no time, Adam and the Hendrix brothers are talking animatedly about Hunger Games vs. Star Wars and everything in between.

Lisa says, "I am so sorry to interrupt the energetic conversation but we wanted to give Adam a chance to ask any final questions to the community as a whole or have any conversations he wanted to with us all around the table. You boys are welcome to stay and join the conversation or go play video games in the other room." Both of the boys say, "We'll stay," and the conversation begins.

Lisa asks Adam, "Is there anything that you have thought of since we've started today that we haven't answered?"

Adam says, "Actually there is. It didn't hit me until we were halfway through the tour, but when we were walking up I noticed that there are different textures as we were walking up the sidewalk. I guess I was too distracted by the flowers when we were first walking up to the house. But, why is that?"

As this point Daniel chimes in and says, "I think I can answer that one for him. The sidewalk is different textures so that it is easier for people with visual impairments to differentiate where they are in the path." Sarah, Daniel's wife, adds, "We have never seen anything quite like that until we started being part of the community, and it wasn't until we moved in that I got a chance to ask Lisa where that came from." Sarah turns to Lisa and says, "Didn't you all tell me that you all saw something like that at the Ed Roberts Campus in Berkley California?"

Lisa says, "Yes we went on a visit there during the planning stages of The Julian Way House and Community. We knew we wanted to integrate that element into the house after our visit."

Adam says, "Thanks. That makes perfect sense when you think about it. I am interested in why you chose Oak Cliff as an area in which to build the house." Lisa looks at Carolyn, smiles, and says, "It wasn't easy and we had lots of prayer and long conversations of discernment. Carolyn, who has been with us from almost the beginning, can tell you."

"Oh yeah, they were long and some of them were loud," Carolyn replies. "Especially when you consider the Oak Cliff neighborhood as a whole. There are some parts that are very accessible and other parts that are not very accessible at all. But, ultimately we chose the Oak Cliff area because of the diversity of the people. You have a number of different economic situations running through the community. And then you have so many generations, from young professionals who move in and out of the neighborhood to residents who have been here for generations and everything in between. We wanted The Julian Way to be a place where everybody is welcome, where we could turn things that others see as barriers into assets and aspects of creativity—whatever they may be."

Adam says, "It sounds like you take being neighbors very seriously."

Alex speaks up and says, "When I first got to The Julian Way it was somewhat difficult. I am a friendly guy but constantly being open and available to neighbors is tough. But I am learning that nobody does this alone. We do this as a family. Whether we are permanent residents or, like the Hendrixes, here for a certain period of time, we are a family, and being neighbors is just another way of living into what God is calling us to be.

The community decides that Adam must stay for dinner to which Adam, being a hungry and poor college student, quickly and joyfully agrees. There is much laughter and much good food as new relationships are forged around the table. By the time Justin and Lisa walk Adam to his car, Adam has agreed to come back the next week and challenge the Hendrix boys to some football on the Xbox. Justin says, "Let us know if you need anything else for your project and we really do want to see you at dinner next Tuesday, and any time you like really, just let us know. Adam says, "Thank you. You are so helpful, and this place is quite the sight to see. I will be back for dinner."

Conclusion

BY NOW, SLIGHTLY OVER one hundred pages into this journey, it might be tempting for you, my dear reader, to ask, "What was the point? Why do I need to know about the struggles of those with disabilities throughout the twentieth century? What difference does engaging in theology through the lens of disability have for my life?" To this I would simply say, this book has been an attempt to add some detail and historical color to the landscape of disability. It can be very easy to boil the ADA down to President Bush, sitting in the Oval Office in 1990, surrounded by those with disabilities and their friends and families, and smiling as he signed this landmark law into reality. If we do this, we can imagine that the ramps, curb cuts, and other markers of physical public access arose *ex nihilo*—from nowhere. Additionally, we can fool ourselves into believing that the heavy lifting of public policy boils down to several months' worth of hearings over the ADA throughout both 1988 and 1989 and that the work of fighting for policy change has already been done. This is the same casual approach to history that leads us to believe that all Martin Luther King Jr. ever did was have a dream, and that can facilitate the lazy approach to theology that allows us to say that all Jesus ever did was die on a cross. I want you to understand, my friends, that on the contrary the disability experience is still carrying echoes of laws like the 1911 Chicago Ugly Law and the living memory of forced institutionalization from the beginning of the early twentieth century through the early 1970s. I want you to understand that the fight for disability civil rights began in earnest in the early 1950s with the government's development of the Department of Health, Education, and Welfare, only to pick up steam in the 1960s and 1970s with folks like Ed Roberts and Justin Dart. The hearings in both 1988 and 1989, that would culminate in the passage of the ADA, are not words in a history book for me and others in the disabled community; they were and still remain moments of living, breathing liberation. I have met activists with scars on their arms from lying on the pavement in front of buses or climbing up bus steps to gain access to public transit. I feel their sacrifice in the breath I use to write this concluding section. I want you, the reader, to feel it as you see the human community in all its diverse shapes and sizes around you.

I invited you to examine theologians such as St. Augustine and Karl Barth to better understand how theologians, although completely contextually relevant and active for their day and time, developed many of the theological assumptions and presuppositions that those with diverse embodiments and other maginalizing conditions find themselves encountering even now as they seek to integrate with the church of today. Let me be very clear: as I stated early on in the theological section of this work, this does not mean that the theologians that we have encountered do not have rich and vital things to say to today's communities of faith. What I am simply inviting us to pay attention to is this: when we fail to appreciate the contextual nature of the words and ideas of theologians like Augustine, it can lead us to presume that when a dominant interpretation of Augustine's theological reflection concerns "the perfection of the human body and mind," he obviously means what we would mean in our modern context, i.e., a mind and body absent of disability. Acknowledging our different contexts helps when looking at Karl Barth and his phrase, "even those who are seriously ill can will to be healthy without any optimism or illusions regarding their condition." Now, I must admit that throughout the course of writing this book, I had and continue to have issues with Barth's line of thinking around this phrase and even in its original context in the late 1930s and early 1940s. However the quote is even more awkward when we, as the people of the church, fail to realize that the notions around disability have shifted dramatically in the latter part of the twentieth century from ones in which disability was primarily associated with illness or sickness, such as in this quote, to more current parlance in which disability is more readily related to physical attributes. For example, I have blue eyes and blond hair and I also live with the condition known as Cerebral Palsy.

What we are left with if we as the church do not understand the contextual dimensions around the theology of disability is a circumstance in which we, the church, will always and forever find ourselves lagging fifteen to twenty years behind the mainstream culture despite our best intentions. What this creates is a dynamic where those persons with a disability continue to feel like a square peg in a round hole. This is why, my friends, the last section of the book was so critically important. I wanted us as a community of Christians to be able to envision a place where the best and fullest life was possible. Where ministry for and with the disabled does not always have to depend on overcoming daily struggles or living into a super-crip narrative in order to be valued or validated. It's up to you and me to notice the gifts and graces of everyone, regardless of physical or developmental embodiments, and to change the narrative into one where those gifts and graces are always needed, wanted, and accepted, regardless of how long it may take or how odd they may appear.

Writing this book has been accompanied by the gradual recognition of a much broader community of humanity than I ever knew before. My hope is, through taking this path with me, you will begin to notice things about the world around you that, perhaps, have always been there but you now see in full color. I have to believe that communities of faith and spaces of acceptance like The Julian Way are actually attainable, real, and physically possible, but for that to be the case, you and I dear friends must take this book and the lessons we have learned together and make them real in our churches, our homes, and our broader communities. Then, and only then, will our ways of faith and our way of life become a community of faith and fullness for all of God's people and become, truly, The Julian Way.

Bibliography

Anderson, Christopher. "Felix Mendelssohn und Friedrich Schleiermacher: zur musikalischen Theologie des Paulus." In *Musik, Kirchenmusik, Theologie: Festschrift Christoph Krummacher zum 65 Geburtstag*, 143–192. Munich: Strube, 2014.

Augustine of Hippo. "*City of God*, XI.16 (470)." In *Disability in the Christian Tradition: A Reader*, edited by Brian Brock and John Swinton, 87. Grand Rapids: Eerdmans, 2012.

——. "*City of God*, XIX.4 (918–24)." In *Disability in the Christian Tradition: A Reader*, edited by Brian Brock and John Swinton, 90–92. Grand Rapids: Eerdmans, 2012

——. *The City of God Against the Pagans*. Edited and translated by R. W. Dyson. Cambridge: Cambridge University Press, 1998.

——. "A Treatise on the Merits and Forgiveness of Sins, and on the Baptism of Infants." In *Disability in the Christian Tradition: A Reader*, edited by Brian Brock and John Swinton, 78–79. Grand Rapids: Eerdmans, 2012.

Barth, Karl. "*Church Dogmatics* III/4, 357–9." In *Disability in the Christian Tradition: A Reader*, edited by Brian Brock and John Swinton, 414–16. Grand Rapids: Eerdmans, 2012.

Berkowitz, Edward. "A Historical Preface to the Americans with Disabilities Act." *Journal of Policy History* 6 (1994): 96–119.

Bérubé, Michael. *Life as We Know It: A Father, a Family, and an Exceptional Child*. New York: Pantheon, 1996.

Bickenbach, J. E., S. Chatterji, E. M. Badley, and T. B. Ustün. "Models of Disablement Universalism and the International Classification of Impairments, Disabilities and Handicaps." *Social Science and Medicine* 48 (1999): 1173–87.

Bonhoeffer, Dietrich. "*Ethics*: Christ, true man." In *Disability in the Christian Tradition: A Reader*, edited by Brian Brock and John Swinton, 387–89. Grand Rapids: Eerdmans, 2012.

——. *Life Together*. London: SCM Press, 1954. Kindle edition.

——. "Sermon for the Evening Worship Service on 2 Corinthians 12:9 (London 1934): 'My Strength Is Made Perfect in Weakness.'" In *Disability in the Christian Tradition: A Reader*, edited by Brian Brock and John Swinton, 372–374. Grand Rapids: Eerdmans, 2012.

Brock, Brian. "Augustine's Hierarchies of Human Wholeness and Their Healing." In *Disability in the Christian Tradition: a Reader*, edited by Brian Brock and John Swinton, 65–100. Grand Rapids: Eerdmans, 2012.

Burks, Courtney L. "Improving Access to Commercial Websites Under the Americans with Disabilities Act and the Twenty-First Century Communications and Video Accessibility Act." *Iowa Law Review* 99 (2013): 363–92.

Bush, George H. W. *Remarks of President George Bush at the Signing of the Americans with Disabilities Act*, 26 July 1990. Equal Employment Opportunity Commission. http://www.eeoc.gov/eeoc/history/35th/videos/ada_signing_text.html.

Couey, J. Blake "The Disabled Body Politic in Isaiah 3:1, 8." *Journal of Biblical Literature* 133 (2014): 95–109.

Creamer, Deborah. *Disability and Christian Theology: Embodied Limits and Constructive Possibilities*. New York: Oxford University Press, 2009.

Dumbreck, Geoff. *Schleiermacher and Religious Feeling*. Paris: Peeters, 2012.

Forstman, Jack. Foreword to *On Religion: Speeches to Its Cultured Despisers*, by Friedrich Schleiermacher, vii–xii. Translated by John Oman. London: Paul, Trench, and Trubner, 1893.

Greenhouse, Carol J. "Ethnography and Democracy: Texts and Contexts in the United States in the 1990s." *Yale Journal of Law and Humanities* 13 (2001): 175–201.

Hall, Amy Laura. "A Ravishing and Restful Sight: Seeing with Julian of Norwich." In *Disability in the Christian Tradition: A Reader*, edited by Brian Brock and John Swinton, 152–83. Grand Rapids: Eerdmans, 2012.

Hauerwas, Stanley. "Community and Diversity: The Tyranny of Normality." In *Critical Reflections on Stanley Hauerwas' Theology of Disability*, edited by John Swinton, 37–44. Binghamton, NY: Haworth, 2004.

———. "The Politics of Gentleness." In *Living Gently in a Violent World: The Prophetic Witness of Weakness*, by Stanley Hauerwas and Jean Vanier. Downers Grove, IL: InterVarsity, 2010. Kindle Edition.

———. "Suffering the Retarded: Should We Prevent Retardation." In *Critical Reflections on Stanley Hauerwas' Theology of Disability*, edited by John Swinton, 87–106. Binghampton, NY: Haworth Pastoral, 2004.

———. "Timeful Friends: Living with the Handicapped." In *Critical Reflections on Stanley Hauerwas' Theology of Disability*, edited by John Swinton, 11–26. Binghampton, NY: Haworth Pastoral, 2004.

Hector, Kevin W. "Actualism and Incarnation: The High Christology of Friedrich Schleiermacher." *International Journal of Systematic Theology* 8 (July 2006): 307–22.

Jones, Jeffrey Douglas. "Enfeebling the ADA: The ADA Amendments Acts of 2008." *Oklahoma Law Review* 62 (2010): 667–700.

Julian of Norwich. *The Revelations*. In *The Complete Julian of Norwich*, edited by Father John-Julian, 63–379. Brewster, MA: Paraclete, 2009.

Junior, Nyasha, and Jeremy Schipper, "Disability Studies and the Bible." In *New Meanings for Ancient Texts*, edited by Steven L. McKenzie and John Kaltner, 21–38. Louisville, : Westminster John Knox, 2013.

———. "Mosaic Disability and Identity in Exodus 4:10; 6:12, 30." *Biblical Interpretation* 16 (2008): 428–41.

Landsman, Gail. "Mothers and Models of Disability." *Journal of Medical Humanities* 26 (2005): 121–39.

Matthews, Nicole. "Contesting Representations of Disabled Children in Picture Books: Visibility, the Body and the Social Model of Disability." *Children's Geographies* 7 (2009): 37–49.

McGrath, Alister E. *Christian Theology: An Introduction*. Oxford: Blackwell, 2001.

McRuer, Robert. "Disability Nationalism in Crip Times." *Journal of Literary and Cultural Studies* 4 (2010): 163–78.

Mitchell, David. *Narrative Prosthesis: Disability and the Dependencies of Discourse*. Ann Arbor: University of Michigan Press, 2000.

Nouwen, Henri. *Adam: God's Beloved*. Maryknoll, NY: Orbis, 1997. Kindle edition.

———. *The Road to Daybreak: A Spiritual Journey*. New York: Image, 1990. Kindle edition.

Reinders, Hans S. "Being with the Disabled: Jean Vanier's Theological Realism." In *Disability in the Christian Tradition: A Reader*, edited by Brian Brock and John Swinton, 467–511. Grand Rapids: Eerdmans, 2012.

Reynolds, Thomas. *Vulnerable Communion: A Theology of Disability and Hospitality*. Grand Rapids: Brazos, 2008.

Schleiermacher, Friedrich. *The Christian Faith*. Edited and translated by H. R. Mackintosh and J. S. Steward. Edinburgh: T. and T. Clark, 1928.

———. *On Religion: Speeches to Its Cultured Despisers*. Translated by John Oman. London: Paul, Trench, and Trubner, 1893.

Spink, Kathryn. *The Miracle, The Message, The Story: Jean Vanier and l'Arche*. Mahwah, NJ: Paulist, 2006. Kindle edition.

Snyder, Sharon, and David Mitchell. *The Cultural Locations of Disability*. Chicago: University of Chicago Press, 2006.

Swinton, John. "The Importance of Being a Creature: Stanley Hauerwas on Disability." In *Disability in the Christian Tradition: A Reader*, edited by Brian Brock and John Swinton, 512–45. Grand Rapids: Eerdmans, 2012.

Taylor, Robin M. "Special Rules for the Church: The 'Ministerial' Exception under the Americans with Disabilities Act." *Dialog* 51 (2012): 224–33.

Union of the Physically Impaired Against Segregation and the Disability Alliance. *Fundamental Principles of Disability*, 1975. http://disability-studies.leeds.ac.uk/files/library/UPIAS-fundamental-principles.pdf.

Vanier, Jean. *Befriending the Stranger*. Mahwah, NJ: Paulist, 2014. Kindle edition.

———. "The Vision of Jesus: Living Peaceably in a Wounded World." In *Living Gently in a Violent World: The Prophetic Witness of Weakness*, by Stanley Hauerwas and Jean Vanier, 59–76. Downers Grove, IL: InterVarsity, 2010. Kindle Edition.

Wood, Donald. "*This* Ability: Barth on the Concrete Freedom of Human Life." In *Disability in the Christian Tradition: A Reader*, edited by Brian Brock and John Swinton, 391–426. Grand Rapids: Eerdmans, 2012.

Young, Jonathan M. *Equality of Opportunity: The Making of the Americans with Disabilities Act*. Washington DC: National Council on Disability, 1997. http://files.eric.ed.gov/fulltext/ED512697.pdf